25✳10-Minute Plays
for Teens

25✳10-Minute Plays
for Teens

Edited by
Lawrence Harbison

APPLAUSE
THEATRE & CINEMA BOOKS
An Imprint of Hal Leonard Corporation

Published in 2014 by Applause Theatre & Cinema Books
An Imprint of Hal Leonard Corporation
7777 West Bluemound Road
Milwaukee, WI 53213

Trade Book Division Editorial Offices
33 Plymouth St., Montclair, NJ 07042

Printed in the United States of America

Book design by John J. Flannery

Library of Congress Cataloging-in-Publication Data

25 10-minute plays for teens / Lawrence Harbison [editor].
     pages cm
 ISBN 978-1-4803-8776-8 (pbk.)
1. One-act plays, American. 2. Teenagers--Drama. I. Harbison, Lawrence,
editor. II. Title: Twenty-five ten-minute plays for teens.
 PS627.O53A145 2014
 812'.04108--dc23
                              2014012023

www.applausebooks.com

CONTENTS

PLAYS FOR HIGH SCHOOLS

PLAYS FOR MIDDLE SCHOOLS

INTRODUCTION

This anthology contains twenty-five terrific new plays, with almost exclusively teenaged characters. Some are for middle-school-aged teens; others are for high school kids. The Contents page identifies which are which. This doesn't mean, though, that high school kids can't do the middle-school plays, and vice versa. All of them have subject matter appropriate for production in schools and that will, I believe, interest teen performers.

It has always been my belief that schools are far too reliant on the "usual suspects"—famous plays from Broadway with few or no teen characters. When I was senior editor for Samuel French, I received many phone calls each year from high school drama directors asking for help in play selection, and I often steered them toward terrific plays we published that were specifically for teens. Some directors were resistant, believing that there was some rule that they could only do a "famous play" from Broadway, largely because it had to be a play that everyone had heard of—to which I replied that they hadn't heard of anything. It's not as if the titles of plays are on the tip of everyone's tongue. And they'll have the same audience, because everyone's going to come to see their kid or their friend in the play. I also expressed my opinion that their kids would have a far better experience doing plays to which they could relate.

Ten-minute plays are being done as bills all over the world, so why not in high schools, too? This volume amounts to one-stop shopping. If you're a teen who wants to take the initiative and do a play with your friends, look no further. If you're a drama teacher, why not do a bill of plays that are in this book, instead of yet another production of *Arsenic and Old Lace*? All of the plays you'll find here are easy to produce, and none require kids to spray paint their hair gray and pretend to be a geezer.

There are wonderful plays in here by some very well-known playwrights (to those who know playwrights) such as Don Nigro, Wendy MacLeod, Constance Congdon, and Jeff Goode, but most are by exciting up-and-comers such as C.S. Hanson, Kayla Cagan, Chad Beckim, Bekah Brunstetter, Merridith Allen, Sharyn Rothstein, and Ashley Cowan. On the title page of each play you will find information as to how you can procure permission to produce it—which is, after all, the point.

Break a leg!

Lawrence Harbison
Brooklyn, NY

25✳10-Minute Plays
for Teens

Plays for High Schools

BAM! KA-POW!

Joe Musso

CHARACTERS
REBECCA, *a young woman.*
TOM, *a young man.*

TIME
The present.

SETTING
REBECCA *and* TOM *are standing onstage.*

> TOM *is holding a superhero comic book. He and* REBECCA *are waiting.*

TOM: How much longer we gonna wait?

> REBECCA *viciously karate kicks* TOM *while yelling "KA-POW!" In pain, he drops to the ground.*

REBECCA: What did I just tell you, Tom?

TOM: To read my comic book.

REBECCA: And?

TOM: To stop asking you "how much longer."

REBECCA: Exactamundo. And did you read your comic book and stop asking "how much longer"?

TOM: No.

REBECCA: Then you deserved what you got.

TOM: I did?

REBECCA: Here, let me help you up.

> REBECCA *helps* TOM *to his feet. As soon as he is standing, she viciously karate kicks again while yelling "WHAMMO." He falls to the floor, writhing in even more pain than before.*

Who was the first costumed villain Wonder Woman ever faced? I need to know for an epic poem I'm writing.

TOM: *Trying unsuccessfully to speak.* D

REBECCA: *Bending down to him.* Huh?

TOM: D

REBECCA: You're not making sense.

TOM: Da. Da. Da.

REBECCA: C'mon. Spit it out.

TOM: Doctor Poison.

REBECCA: *Standing straight.* Cool.

> TOM *makes a half-hearted attempt at standing and falls back to the ground.*

You okay?

> TOM *shakes his head "no."*

Are you Bucky by any chance?

> TOM *shakes his head "no."*

'Cause Bucky was Captain America's sidekick, and sidekicks are cool.

TOM: *With effort.* Can you spare some chewing gum?

REBECCA: Sure.

> *She hands* TOM *a wrapped red gum ball.*

I gotta warn you, though. That gum barely has any flavor at all.

TOM: Yeah?

> *He unwraps the red gum ball and pops it into his mouth. He begins chewing it. Spitting out the gum; his tongue is on fire:*

AAAAAAHHHHHHHHH!!!!!!

REBECCA: I lied. That was actually habanero gum. You know, made from those scalding hot habenero peppers.

TOM: *Pleading.* Water.

REBECCA: I'm creating a new superhero, Habenero Man.

TOM: *Pleading.* Water.

REBECCA: He can breathe fire.

TOM: *Pleading.* Water.

REBECCA: His sidekick will be Banana Pepper Girl.

TOM: *Pleading.* Water.

REBECCA: Sidekicks are soooo cool. Have I told you that?

TOM: *Pleading.* Water.

REBECCA: Water? You must like Aqua Man.

TOM: *Pleading.* Please. Water.

REBECCA: Aqua Man was one of the founders of the Justice League.

TOM *faints.*

REBECCA: Did you just faint, or are you playing possum?

She kicks TOM*'s leg.*

Guess you really did faint.

She exits and returns with a cup of water, which she splashes on TOM*'s face.* TOM *is jolted awake.*

TOM: Water!

REBECCA: Yep. That's what you got.

TOM: More. Water.

REBECCA: Sorry. That was the last of it.

TOM *manages to stand.*

You look sorta sickly. Are you okay?

TOM *nods that he is okay.*

Are you a mime? I really, really hate mimes. Last mime I came across, I kicked him.

TOM *cowers.*

TOM: Rebecca, can you just chill for a second?

REBECCA: Chill?

TOM: Yes, chill.

REBECCA: Okay.

TOM: Thank you.

REBECCA: You're welcome. *Pause.* You can relax. I'm done kicking you.

TOM *tentatively relaxes. A pause.*

TOM: Whew.

REBECCA *viciously kicks* TOM *again, this time while yelling "HI-YA!" He falls, in tears, unable to breathe.*

REBECCA: *After he writhes a bit.* That floor's filthy. Want me to help you up?

TOM: *Without sound. Mouthing the word.* No.

REBECCA: Cool, I could read your lips just now. *Pause.* Do you have any rare comic books? Huh? Do ya?

TOM: *Struggling.* No.

REBECCA: I do. My grandpappy gave me a 1947 copy of the *Blonde Phantom.* Ever heard of *Blonde Phantom* comic books?

TOM: *Still struggling.* No.

REBECCA: The Blonde Phantom's this awesome crime-fighter chick. She's absolutely gorgeous. Unlike She-Hulk, who is ugly with a capital "U." You ever read any *She-Hulk* comics?

TOM: *Still struggling.* No.

REBECCA: There's this one comic book, started in the nineteen-sixties, called the *Inferior Five.* You ever read the *Inferior Five?*

TOM: *Still struggling.* No.

REBECCA: One of the Inferior Five is named Dumb Bunny. She's stupid but super strong. You wouldn't want to get on Dumb Bunny's bad side.

TOM *moans in pain.*

REBECCA: What's wrong? You're not your usual cheerful self.

TOM: Please.

REBECCA: Please what?

TOM: Stop.

REBECCA: Stop what?

TOM: Kicking.

REBECCA: Kicking what?

TOM:: Me.

REBECCA: Please stop kicking you?

TOM: Yes.

REBECCA: Why?

TOM: What?

REBECCA: Why should I stop kicking you?

TOM: 'Cause.

REBECCA: 'Cause why?

TOM: It hurts.

REBECCA: Not me.

TOM: You?

REBECCA: It doesn't hurt me.

TOM: You?

REBECCA: Actually, it feels great, unleashing all that energy.

TOM: I'm . . .

REBECCA: Yes?

TOM: In some real pain.

REBECCA: Sorry—no pain, no gain. Truth and justice rarely win the day without a little violence.

TOM: Truth and justice?

REBECCA: I find that truth and justice is a common theme in comic books.

TOM: I think . . .

Slight pause.

REBECCA: Uh-huh?

TOM: That . . .

Slight pause.

REBECCA: Yeah?

TOM: You're crazy.

REBECCA: Yep, I'm crazy for comic books. In fact, Batman was born in a 1939 issue of *Detective Comics*. It only cost ten cents. Ten cents, I tell you.

TOM: I'm leaving.

REBECCA: Now?

TOM: Yes.

REBECCA: Right now?

TOM: Yes.

REBECCA: Where will you go?

TOM: I don't know, and I don't care.

REBECCA: But I was just about to give a lecture on the Curse of Kordax.

TOM: I don't care about the Curse of Kordax, or any other curse.

He begins to exit.

REBECCA: Wait!

TOM: *Stopping.* What?

REBECCA: I'll miss you.

TOM: Well, I won't miss you.

He exits.

REBECCA: *After him:*

Who will I talk to about comic books?

Slight pause, waving after him:

Bye.

To audience:

You know, he's kinda cute. If you squint your eyes a little when you look at him.

More quietly: He never actually came out and said it, but I think he likes me.

She puts on a yellow cape and a superhero eye mask. To audience:

About the Curse of Kordax. In ancient Atlantis there lived an evil tyrant named Kordax. He had blond hair and could communicate with marine life. Because he was evil and a tyrant, the people of Atlantis hated him. So much so, that if you were born in Atlantis with blond hair like Kordax, you were left to die as a baby. Aquaman was born in Atlantis and had blond hair. Therefore, he was left to die as a baby. Still, he overcame his blond hair and grew up to help start the Justice League. The moral of the story: never give up. Always fight for truth and justice, no matter what.

TOM *returns.*

TOM: Who are you, masked princess?

REBECCA: I'm Banana Pepper Girl. Together with Habanero Man, I fight for truth and justice.

TOM: Cool.

REBECCA: And my superhuman power is kicking.

She violently kicks TOM while yelling "WA-BAM!" He falls to the ground.

TOM: Banana Pepper Girl, I love you.

Smiling, she strikes a triumphant superhero pose. Blackout.

END OF PLAY

CLUB FOOT

Wendy MacLeod

CHARACTERS

JOSH: 17, *an ordinary teenager with a clubfoot.*
ELLA: 17, *an ordinary teenager.*

TIME

July 4, the present.

SETTING

A country club bathroom with old-fashioned wallpaper, botanical prints on the wall, and an overstuffed feminine pouffe. There are stacks of pink hand towels by each sink.

NOTE: The directors and actors are free to update or change the movie-star names in parentheses to make them more appropriate to the situation.

> ELLA, *a teen-aged girl, bursts through the door, followed by a limping* JOSH, *an ordinary teenager with a clubfoot.*

JOSH: Don't run away from me.

ELLA: You can't be in here.

JOSH: Talk to me.

ELLA: I've tried.

JOSH: You don't have to do this.

ELLA: I do.

JOSH: Just because I don't look like (James Franco) or . . .

ELLA: I don't even like him . . .

JOSH: (Leonardo di Caprio) . . .

ELLA: Why would I have chosen you to begin with if I cared about your foot . . . ?

JOSH: Maybe you pitied me.

ELLA: Oh don't be. Pitied. God.

JOSH: Maybe you expected it to be romantic when it was actually just slow.

ELLA: Oh right because that's how I choose my boyfriends. Based on speed.

JOSH: Boyfriends?

ELLA: You're not my first boyfriend . . .

JOSH: Who's your next boyfriend?

ELLA: I don't know.

JOSH: I think you do . . .

ELLA: Just . . . go!

JOSH: You don't want to tell me.

ELLA: I don't have to tell you. We broke up.

> JOSH *picks up one of the hand towels stacked by the sink.*

JOSH: Who washes these?

> ELLA *makes a "how should I know?" gesture.*

A few rich people dry their hands once and they have to do an entire load of laundry.

ELLA: It's their job.

JOSH: And they should be grateful.

ELLA: Maybe they should. Maybe they don't speak English and it's this or some meatpacking plant . . .

JOSH: *Tossing aside the towel.* God I hate pink.

ELLA: I didn't choose the towels. It's not my club.

JOSH: But you're not like boycotting it.

ELLA: Why should I?

JOSH: Because it's classist and dated and discriminatory . . .

ELLA: Because you don't belong it's discriminatory . . .

JOSH: I don't want to belong.

ELLA: Then maybe you should leave.

JOSH: Not till you . . .

ELLA: What?

JOSH: Speak kindly to me.

ELLA: I don't feel kindly towards you right now.

JOSH: Can I see you tomorrow?

ELLA: No.

JOSH: If I can see you tomorrow, I'll go.

ELLA: Don't pressure me.

JOSH: I need to know that I'm going to see you.

ELLA: You need to have other friends!

JOSH: I have other friends. *A moment.* I have other friends.

ELLA: I really have to pee.

JOSH: Pee then.

ELLA: I'm not going to pee while you're standing here!

JOSH: I've heard you pee before.

ELLA: I need some privacy.

JOSH: So you can make your little secret phone call.

ELLA: What phone call?

JOSH: To Jackson Keading.

ELLA: Who?

JOSH: I saw you.

ELLA: Were you spying?

JOSH: Lying on the blanket. Looking up at the sexually symbolic fireworks.

ELLA: Why are they symbolic?! It's the Fourth of July.

JOSH: You told me you were busy.

ELLA: I said I was going to the club.

JOSH: You just forgot to mention . . .

ELLA: I ran into him.

JOSH: *Mocking, feigning surprise.* "Oh Jackson, do you belong to this club?"

ELLA: It's really hard to find you attractive when you're being so pathetic . . .

JOSH: Jackson Keading is a dick. He wouldn't even pay for Tricia's abortion . . .

ELLA: How do you even know that?

JOSH: And then he broke up with her. So, you know, you sure know how to pick 'em.

The door opens. Someone peeks in and then backs out before we see them.

ELLA: *Gesturing toward the woman who left.* This is a ladies' room!

JOSH: I'll leave when you leave.

ELLA: You're being such a stalker!

JOSH: And you're being such a fucking girl deriving her sense of self-worth from whatever jock deigns to sleep with her.

ELLA: Okay, I'll leave . . .

JOSH: *Stepping in front of her.* Don't forget your little pink towel.

ELLA: I expected you to be nicer than other people, but people with disabilities can be assholes, too . . .

JOSH: Obviously . . .

ELLA: I mean look at Richard III!

JOSH: He's my role model!

ELLA: I don't like Jackson Keading because he's a jock. I like him because he texted me "Good Night." Like out of the blue. And said "No need to text back." Whereas you need like seventy-five texts a day or you freak out!

JOSH: That was one day, when I had legitimate reasons to think you might not have gotten my texts . . .

ELLA: Let me by.

JOSH: I thought you had to pee.

ELLA: I don't have to anymore.

JOSH: I'll wait in the hall.

ELLA: You can't wait in the hall. You can't be anywhere. You're not a member here.

Beat. Her phone dings with a text.

JOSH: Whoever could that be?

ELLA: *Glancing down, rolling her eyes.* My mom.

He grabs the phone out of her hand.

Give me my fucking phone!

He sees the text is from Jackson. He crumples, sits down on the pouffe.

JOSH: I don't have any other friends.

ELLA: *Torn.* You have friends . . .

JOSH: Who? Who do I have?

A moment. Then ELLA *goes out the door.*

END OF PLAY

INTERPRETING A DREAM
Judy Klass

CHARACTERS

ARIEL: *a confident, hip, high school senior who is secure enough about her popularity to try to help out a nerd in trouble. Her clothes, hair, etcetera, should reflect her level of cool.*

IVANIA: *a shy, sensitive girl who is lost in a dream world. She is the same age as* IVANIA *but appears younger. She wears a blouse with a peter pan collar, with either brand x jeans or a simple, dark polyester skirt.*

MR. MILLER: *a high school principal who is in his forties. He is stuffy, though he sees himself as able to "rap" with kids and be one of the gang.*

TIME

The present.

SETTING

MR. MILLER*'s office, and then* IVANIA*'s dream bedroom.* IVANIA *sits sullen, slumped in a chair in the principal's office.* ARIEL, *in the chair beside her, tries to cheer her up and reason with her.*

ARIEL: So, listen, don't be scared or nothing like that. I'll try to do some damage control for you.

> IVANIA *does not respond.*

Listen, I been meaning to tell you—if you want to go to the mall some time, together, that would be cool. We could go with Sandra and Elise, or whatever. I could just go with you. Pick out some new clothes. I'd be happy to do that.

> IVANIA *looks down—expressionless—at her clothes, then over at pretty, hip* ARIEL.

I'm not saying you have to spend a fortune, and buy all Calvin Klein and DKNY or whatever. *Oiste? No es necesario a comprar muchas cosas, es possible a llevar mucho que ya tu tienes . . .* I just mean, like, if you want to fit in more. Don't take it the wrong way.

> IVANIA *glances around the room.*

¿Que piensas?

IVANIA: *Shrugs.* Nada.

ARIEL: *Nada.* Great. *Espero que tu insanidad no me dañe. Mira, quiero ayudarte, pero tienes que intentar ayudarte tu mismo.* You gotta try to help yourself!

IVANIA *again shrugs.*

He's not such a bad guy. *No es mal hombre. El cree que un dialogo,* you know, a "dialogue" *puede resolver todo. Pero, la cosa es para parecer escuchar su consejo—y no a mostrar miedo!* Don't look like you're scared!

IVANIA: *No tengo miedo.*

ARIEL: *Annoyed.* ¿Y porque no?

> MR. MILLER *enters. He gives the girls a big, reassuring smile, and moves to shake hands with both of them.* IVANIA *lets him lift her limp hand, but applies no pressure to his.*

MR. MILLER: Hello, ladies. Thank you for waiting.

> *He moves behind his desk, sits.*

And, Ariel, thank you for volunteering to help out here.

ARIEL: No problem, Mr. Miller. I'm glad to do it.

MR. MILLER: I think this is the third time we've had you in here interpreting for someone, is that right?

ARIEL: Fourth time.

MR. MILLER: Well. If this keeps up, you can go to work for the UN after college.

> ARIEL *smiles at his little joke.* IVANIA *remains expressionless.*
>
> *You are planning to go to college, aren't you?*

ARIEL: Yes, sir, I've applied to five schools where I maybe got a shot.

MR. MILLER: Well, that's terrific. You know, I've heard really wonderful things about you from Mrs. Caldicott.

> *Clasps hands on desk. He pronounces the first syllable of "Ivania" the same as "eye."*

So. Does Ivania know . . .

IVANIA: *Sharply corrects him, with an "ee" sound*: Eevania.

MR. MILLER: *Taken aback, pronounces it correctly*: Eevania. I'm sorry. *To* ARIEL: Does Ivania know why she's been sent to my office?

ARIEL: *To* IVANIA. *Entiendes porqué estamos aquí?*

> IVANIA *shrugs.*

MR. MILLER: We understand that she's having trouble adjusting, and that a new country can seem big and scary. We're not trying to gang up on her here. We want to try to help her, be her friend.

ARIEL: *El dice que es tu amigo, quiere ayudarte. Hazlo más facil!*

IVANIA *shrugs.*

MR. MILLER: Aha. Ariel, do you have any idea what's going on with her?

ARIEL: Oh, I don't know. I think she's just sad, she misses her country, maybe she misses her old friends.

MR. MILLER: Well, but she's been over here since the start of the year. And apparently she's making no effort to adjust or learn the language. Explain to her, please, that when we say "bilingual education" we do mean it. "Bilingual" means both languages, not just Spanish.

ARIEL: *Dice que "bilingual" significa ambos idiomas. Porque no puedes hablar inglés?*

IVANIA: *No me gusta.*

ARIEL: *Qué?*

IVANIA: *Es un idioma feo, un ruido, con sonidos como la ladrido de un perro. No tiene lógica. Ni ritmo. Es feo como este país es feo, y tosco . . . y cruel.*

MR. MILLER: What did she say?

ARIEL: *Uncertain how much to tell him.* Um, she says that English is very hard for her to learn. It's, uh, different from Spanish . . .

MR. MILLER: But did she just say we were being cruel to her?

ARIEL: Oh, no . . . she's saying that . . . she doesn't like English and the U.S. so much.

MR. MILLER: But she's here now. And frankly . . . I'll level with you Ariel. This is something I don't understand about a lot of our Hispanic students—and obviously you're an exception. If I go on a trip to visit a foreign country, I at least use Berlitz or Rosetta Stone first. I mean, I would make an effort to learn the language, to say, "How much does that cost?" Or "Where is a good hotel?" It's just polite. I wouldn't expect them to speak like me. And yet we have students here . . . and of course I don't mean you, your English is wonderful . . .

ARIEL: Well, I was born here. I'm an American.

MR. MILLER: Well, all right then, you see? But the ones who weren't born here, they're not just here on vacation. Most of them are planning to live out their lives here. And yet so many just won't make an effort. And I suppose, in their homes, in their neighborhoods, they don't have to. But what about when they get a job, out in the real world?

ARIEL: Plenty of jobs you don't need English for, Mr. Miller. I mean, you're making a really good point, don't get me wrong . . .

MR. MILLER: But earlier generations of immigrants, they learned the language. They had to.

ARIEL: Well, you know. First generation?

MR. MILLER: *Annoyed at being challenged.* First generation, second generation—they learned it. This is a nation of immigrants, yes. But in order to be united, we need to have one language in common, a lingua franca, a coin of the realm. The name for the United States in Latin is *E pluribus unum*, did you know that?

ARIEL: No, sir.

MR. MILLER: "In many one." And the common language makes us one. That's what I don't understand about a student like this. Her attitude. What does she think about when the teachers are trying to help her with her English?

ARIEL: *To IVANIA. Qué pasa cuando las clases son en inglés? Porqué no lo aprendes?*

IVANIA: *Porque no vale la pena. Generalmente, no estoy allí en el aula.*

ARIEL: *Dondé estas?*

IVANIA: *Estoy en mi cuarto en mi casa. Mi casa de verdad, no ese pequeño apartamento feo donde vivimos ahora en esta ciudad sucia. En mi casa de verdad, en mi país, tengo una vista de los árboles alrededor del patio. Huelo las hojas y las flores, y siento el silencio y el viento. Escucho los discos de mi abuelita. Y . . . eso es todo.*

MR. MILLER: What did she say?

ARIEL: *Again, trying to be diplomatic.* She . . . gets distracted during class. She feels homesick, she misses her old house, the courtyard. Stuff like that.

MR. MILLER: Well, sure. I can understand that. But her parents decided to come here to build a better life, right? They wanted her to be an American. Doesn't she owe it to them to try?

ARIEL: *To* IVANIA. *Mira, si tus padres quieren vivir aquí, tu debes aceptar esta cultura, dice.*

IVANIA: No.

ARIEL: No?

IVANIA: *En mi propio país, por supuesto tuve mucho cariño y respeto de mis padres. Pero eso era antes de su traición a mí y a mí país. Allí tenían trabajos admirables, aquí son mugre. Ellos piensan que es un cambio bueno, yo no.*

ARIEL: Ay.

MR. MILLER: Well?

ARIEL: She's mad at her parents that they moved here. She doesn't respect them so much anymore.

MR. MILLER: I see. So, she refuses to learn English in order to get back at them. Well, we all go through a phase when we're angry at our parents, when they make choices we don't understand. *Smiling, affable.* Tell her that the great writer Mark Twain used to fight with his father when he was growing up.

ARIEL: *To* IVANIA. *Habla de Mark Twain. Creo que va hacer un chiste.*

MR. MILLER: And he said, when I turned twenty-one, I was amazed to find that my father had suddenly become so much smarter!

He chuckles. ARIEL *smiles, and urges* IVANIA*:*

ARIEL: *Si, lo hizo. Algo aburrido sobre el padre del escritor. Por lo menos, sonrie!*

IVANIA *remains expressionless, staring at* MR. MILLER *without seeing him.*

You know, I think she's a really messed-up person, with a lot on her mind.

To IVANIA*:*

Mira, estas en un aprieto! El es el principal del colegio!

IVANIA: *Shrugs.* Y, pues?

ARIEL: *Llamara a tus padres. Quieres eso?*

IVANIA: *No importa.*

ARIEL: Oh no?

IVANIA: *No. No creo en* él. *No creo en mis padres. No creo en tí. Todo* *esto es un sueño que no significa nada, mi vida real es en mi pueblo, en mi casa vendida, donde hay belleza y suavidad, donde las personas son gentiles y no son vulgares . . . todo esto no existe.*

MR. MILLER: What is she telling you?

ARIEL: *Uncertain once more how to tell him.* She says, um . . . we don't really exist.

MR. MILLER: *Surprised.* What?

ARIEL: She feels . . . she sees all this as a dream. She wants to be back in her country.

MR. MILLER: I see. Perhaps the school counselor should have a talk with her. It's a shame that he really doesn't speak Spanish. We might need you to interpret for us again, and I don't want to keep pulling you out of class, so maybe we can arrange some kind of meeting after school. Do you play any team sport?

ARIEL: No, not right now. And I'm not doing any clubs.

Meanwhile, from the moment MR. MILLER *mentions the school counselor and he and* ARIEL *begin to talk, a Spanish ballad, from the forties or fifties, begins to play. It should be a love song about loyalty, about not forgetting a loved one.* IVANIA *looks off to the side of the stage, previously in darkness, where a bed with a nicely patterned blanket is revealed. There is a potted plant on a table by the bed, and books in Spanish on the table and the bed. The other two do not see it.*

MR. MILLER: So that might work out. I think I'd better have a meeting with her parents first. Again, it's so hard, when the parents don't speak English, to find out about a child's emotional state, what's going on in the home. I don't suppose you know the family?

ARIEL: No, I don't know them. You know, I see her around, we have homeroom together, and at lunch a couple of times I invited her to come sit with me and my friends. But she just keeps to herself.

As the conversation in English continues, the music grows louder, drowning the English out, and IVANIA *rises and crosses to the bed. The others do not notice—*MR. MILLER *or* ARIEL *occasionally indicates* IVANIA*'s seat, as if she's still in it.*

MR. MILLER: Well, her parents really should get her some kind of professional help, but of course that costs money. There are some community counseling services in Spanish, though. I'll have to have my secretary look into it.

We can barely hear him by this point as his conversation with ARIEL fades; IVANIA sits on the bed, and parts imaginary curtains as if looking out on a courtyard, and finally we see her smile and look happy. The song swells, and the lights grow brighter over this area and go down over the principal's office as the lights fade.

END OF PLAY

JAX-IN-A-BOX

Jeff Goode

Jax-in-a-Box was first presented by SkyPilot Theatre Company of Los Angeles (www.skypilottheatre.com) on September 21, 2013, at Determined to Succeed L.A. (www.dtsla.org), under the direction of Nicole B. Adkins, with the following cast:

JACKSON: Jason Kobielus
DARIUS: Jude Evans

CHARACTERS
DARIUS: *14 to 18, an older brother.*
JACKSON: *12 to 16, a younger brother.*

TIME
The present. Around lunchtime.

SETTING
A few blocks away from the school.

> *Lights go up on a large cardboard box. Enter* DARIUS, *dribbling a basketball. He notices the box, decides to ignore it, at first. After a while, though, he dribbles closer.*

DARIUS: Is that you, Jax?

JACKSON: *From inside the box.* Go away.

DARIUS: What are you doing?

JACKSON: I said, "Keep walking!"

DARIUS: Aren't you supposed to be in school?

JACKSON: Aren't you?

> DARIUS *dribbles in silence.*

DARIUS: Does your mom know you're in a box?

JACKSON: What do you care? You're not my brother no more.

DARIUS: No, but I bet your mom'd care if she found out you was cuttin' class. *Pause for effect.* Might even give me a reward for turning you in.

JACKSON: I'm not going back to that school!

DARIUS: I hear that.

JACKSON: Ever.

DARIUS: I thought you liked school.

JACKSON: Who told you that?

DARIUS: You get good grades.

JACKSON: Ha!

DARIUS: Better than I get.

JACKSON: That basketball gets better grades than you get.

DARIUS: Don't make me come in there, Jackson.

JACKSON: The only thing I like about that school is from now until three o'clock, everyone in the world that hates me is inside that building. And as long as I stay out of it, they can't get me.

DARIUS: Kids pickin' on you again?

JACKSON: Again? They don't stop, Darius!

DARIUS: So how do you think it's gonna go if they see you hiding in a box?

JACKSON: They can't see me, if I'm in here. That's the point, stupid.

DARIUS: You gotta watch your mouth.

JACKSON: The only thing they're gonna see is some idiot skippin' class so he can talk to a box.

DARIUS: All right, that's it, you're comin' out!

DARIUS *plunges his hand into the box. And quickly pulls it back out.*

Ow! You cut me!

JACKSON: I scratched you. Don't be a baby.

DARIUS: I'll show you who's a baby!

He plunges both hands in the box. And just as quickly pulls them back out.

Ow! Knock it off!

JACKSON: I'm not comin' out!

DARIUS: Fine, stay in there.

JACKSON: I will!

DARIUS: You need to cut your fingernails.

JACKSON: I did. And then I sharpened them.

DARIUS: You what?? Why'd you do that?

JACKSON: Cuz it's the only thing keeps people from grabbin' at me.

DARIUS: That's stupid.

JACKSON: You gonna stick your hand in here again?

DARIUS: No.

JACKSON: Then it's working.

DARIUS *dribbles, considers leaving.*

DARIUS: You can't stay in there forever, Jackson.

JACKSON: Not forever. Just until I graduate high school.

DARIUS: You're not gonna graduate if you don't come outta your box.

JACKSON: All I need is a D-minus.

DARIUS: Everybody hates school, Jax, but we all gotta go. You think I like it in school?

JACKSON: You don't like it cuz you're bad at it. I don't like it cuz they all want me dead.

DARIUS: What? Nobody wants you dead.

JACKSON: Then I don't know where I heard it.

DARIUS: You think the whole school's tryin' to kill you?

JACKSON: I didn't say that. I said they want me to die. They say it to my face.

DARIUS: They don't say you should die.

JACKSON: And send me links to suicide kids like I should take a hint.

DARIUS: You're makin' that up.

JACKSON: I'm not makin' it up, Darius! Just cuz you don't wanna see it, don't mean it's not happening! That's why they do it, Darius! Cuz they think you're okay with it.

DARIUS: I never said it was okay.

JACKSON: No, you don't have to say nothin'. Just stand there and watch. *Pause.* Be nice if somebody had my back.

DARIUS: So all this is cuz you're afraid to go to school?

JACKSON: I'm not afraid!

DARIUS: You're hidin' in a box.

JACKSON: I tried to go. I can't. I get sick to my stomach.

DARIUS: You get sick being at school?

JACKSON: It's like I can't breathe. My hands start shaking. I tried to go today and I had to throw up in the parking lot.

DARIUS: Aw, no, yuck. Did anybody see you?

JACKSON: I don't know. I ran away.

DARIUS: Well, I guess you did the right thing. You don't want people finding out about that.

JACKSON: And the farther away I ran, the better I felt. Until I got here and I crawled in this box. And now I'm fine. As long as I stay in here, I'm fine.

DARIUS: You're not fine. You're in a box. This isn't fine.

JACKSON: It's quiet. There's nobody here to tell me what they think of me.

DARIUS: You gotta come outta there sometime, Jax. Look, you don't see me skippin' school just cuz I don't keep up in my classes. And all my teachers ridin' me cuz I can't get the same grades as my little brother.

JACKSON *pokes his head out of the box for the first time.*

JACKSON: *Suspicious.* You're right. You don't care about any of that.

DARIUS: That's what I'm sayin'.

JACKSON: So why are you here?

DARIUS: What?

JACKSON: You don't care what anybody thinks of you or me or your grades. So why are you outta school?

DARIUS: I'm not. I came looking for you.

JACKSON: No, you didn't.

DARIUS: Your mom sent me.

JACKSON: Why don't you call her, then? Tell her you found me.

DARIUS: I don't know her number.

JACKSON: You're here cuz you skipped outta school. What are you up to? If they sent you to mess with me, I'll scratch you.

DARIUS: Now, stop it! Nobody sent me.

JACKSON: I'm callin' my mom.

DARIUS: All right, stop . . . Look, I accidentally . . . I accidentally asked out the wrong girl, okay?

JACKSON: What wrong girl?

DARIUS: Shaundra Kelly.

JACKSON: Ha! That's never gonna happen!

DARIUS: Thanks, bro.

JACKSON: So what did she say?

DARIUS: What do you think she said?

JACKSON: I think she smacked you and told you to step off.

DARIUS: She told me she'd think about it.

JACKSON: Ha! You're such an idiot! That means "no."

DARIUS: She said she'd talk to me at lunch.

JACKSON: It's almost lunchtime now. What're you doing here?

DARIUS: I'm not goin' in that cafeteria.

JACKSON: Why not?

DARIUS: Cuz you're right, all right? It's never gonna happen. And I don't need her laughin' at me in front of all her friends.

JACKSON: That would be funny.

DARIUS: Watch it.

JACKSON: You gotta eat some time, Darius.

DARIUS: I hafta cut weight for track anyway.

JACKSON: So you're afraid of a girl.

DARIUS: No, I'm not.

JACKSON: You're not in school, cuz you're afraid of a little girl.

DARIUS: You shut up. Come out of there.

He tries to grab JACKSON, *who ducks back down in the box.*

Ow! Stop scratching!

JACKSON: Stop grabbing!

DARIUS *glares at the box. From inside the box:*

So what are you gonna do? Drop out of school?

DARIUS: I wish.

JACKSON: Over Shaundra Kelly?

DARIUS: Well, I can't now.

JACKSON: Yeah, your dad'll kill you, missing class over nothing.

DARIUS: Forget that. Your mom'll kill me if she thinks I gave you the idea.

JACKSON *emerges again.*

JACKSON: Hey, that's right. That's exactly what she's gonna think if she finds out.

DARIUS: You better not be getting any ideas.

JACKSON: I could stay here all week and not get in trouble if she thought you put me up to it.

DARIUS: You better not.

JACKSON: Oh, man, and your dad would hear it.

DARIUS: You try it and you'll have one more person in that school that hates you.

JACKSON *goes back into his box.*

Naw, come on, I'm sorry. I didn't mean it.

After a while, JACKSON *sticks his head back out.*

JACKSON: You're gonna have to go back, y'know.

DARIUS: I know that.

JACKSON: Can't stay out here forever. You look like an idiot. People think you're afraid.

DARIUS: Yeah, what about you?

JACKSON: There's worse things than looking like an idiot.

DARIUS: Tell you what. Why don't we both go back?

JACKSON: What good's that gonna do?

DARIUS: Prob'ly nothing.

JACKSON: Well, then let's not. Are you crazy?

DARIUS: What if I told you from now on I'll try to have your back?

JACKSON: You think that's gonna stop 'em?

DARIUS: Prob'ly not. But it's something.

JACKSON: What if I don't believe you?

DARIUS: I guess that's fair.

JACKSON: But I guess it's worth a try.

DARIUS: Gotta start somewhere. Come on.

He turns to go. JACKSON *stands up in his box, and eventually follows.*

You gonna lose the box?

JACKSON: Don't rush me.

DARIUS: Okay. But I'm not goin' in school with you like that.

JACKSON: We got four more blocks.

DARIUS: I'm just sayin'.

JACKSON: Don't rush me!

Lights fade.

END OF PLAY

LAST FIRST KISS

Chad Beckim

CHARACTERS
GABBY: *17, female.*
PETER: *17, male.*

TIME
The present.

SETTING
Any suburban high school. Anywhere that there are suburban high schools.

> *A high school bathroom. Muffled eighties music, a la Bon Jovi's "Livin' on a Prayer," almost drowns out the sounds of a young woman crying in the stalls. Almost, but not quite. The bathroom door opens halfway, the music flooding the space. PETER peeks his head in.*

PETER: Gabby? Gab, you in there?

> *Crying. PETER slowly works himself into the bathroom, allowing the door to close behind him. He is dressed in a rental tux. His cheeks are flush, but there's something incredibly electric about him. He's shining.*

Gabby? Gab? Mrs. Marks is out there rockin' out to "Livin' on a Prayer" and I thought you should see it. It's really a sight to behold.

> *Beat. He works his way further in and leans against the sink.*

You know this one? When I was a kid, I really loved this song . . . my dad would take my brothers and me roller skating on Saturdays to this place that would only play seventies and eighties music, and they would play this song and I would just fly around the place, you know, like I was the only one out there. Practically doing air guitar and all that. This song really used to rock. It sucks that it's turned into this drunk-college-boy-douchebag thing. *Beat.* Anyway, I thought that I would come in here and join you, you know, find my date and make sure that she's okay. Gab? "Tony the Tiger" was asking for you. *Joking.* Gabby's ggggrrrreeeeeeEEEAAAAATTTTT!

GABBY: Go away, Peter!

PETER: Gabby . . .

GABBY: Go away, you asshole.

PETER: Gab . . .

GABBY: Don't call me Gab!

PETER: What am I supposed to call you? Gabby, then? *No answer.* Gabrielle?

Sounds it out as "Gab-ree-elle?" with bad French accent:

Gab-ree-elle, come vees me, we make bee-you-tee-ful music en Parees by zee reever . . . *Silence.* I'm sorry. Bad timing.

GABBY: *Tearful, pleading.* Please go away, Peter. Please? Go. Away.

PETER: I . . . I'm sorry, Gab.

GABBY: I told you not to call me that!

PETER: What am I supposed to call you? That's how I know you— that's all I know. Gab. Not Gabby, not Gabrielle, just . . .

GABBY: No, you obviously don't know me. You—sycophant!

Beat.

PETER: Wait, what? What did you just call me?

GABBY: Syco—sorry. Regents. It means . . .

PETER: I know what it means. I just wanted you to say something other than "Go away" or "Stop."

GABBY: You're a liar. Like, this ridiculously huge fucking liar!

PETER: I'm so, so sorry, Gab. I feel terrible. You have no idea.

GABBY: Whatever. It didn't look like you were feeling terrible. It actually really looked like you were enjoying yourself!

PETER: Okayyyy . . . well, if we're going to have this conversation, would you at least consider coming out of the stall?

Beat.

GABBY: I can't.

PETER: What do you mean, you can't?

GABBY: I can't, Peter. I look like a, whatever, a zombie or something. Go away.

PETER: What are you talking about?

GABBY: How can you be this dense? I'm crying? My makeup is running, you moron. My eyes have these huge, dark circles around them.

PETER: I'm sure it's fine.

GABBY: It's not fine, Peter. It's not fine at all. Don't be so oblivious. Do you have any clue how much money I spent on this stupid dress? This, stupid . . . hair? My aunt had her friend from Mary Kay do my makeup . . . it's all over my face now. I look like, like, "The Walking Dead."

PETER: What's wrong with that? We like that show.

GABBY: They're dead, Peter!

PETER: Okay, yeah, but we still like the show. Come out. Please? Come out so we can talk.

A long beat. Gabby *comes out. She does look a little "Walking Dead-ish," but is undeniably pretty.*

See? It's not so bad.

GABBY: Why are you such a liar?

Scratches at her wrist.

This thing is really irritating me!

She tears her corsage off and throws it at him.

Take this! It's probably poison ivy or something.

Beat. She glares at him.

Tell me.

PETER: Gab . . .

GABBY: Don't "Gab" me. You don't deserve it.

PETER: What do you want me to say?

GABBY: You wanted me out here, so say something. Say anything. Just don't stand there with that stupid dopey look on your face.

PETER: *Painfully sincere.* I'm sorry.

GABBY: Accepted. Go away.

PETER: Don't do that. I mean, don't be . . . like that.

GABBY: Every day, I see these girls—pretty girls, smart girls, like my friends, my sisters, their friends—all these girls surrounded by these stupid, selfish, asshole boys. I see all of these girls get treated like shit every single day, and just, take it. Day in, day out, just take this bullshit nonsense. And every day it made me more and more determined not to be like that. Me, thinking, "No way that's going to happen to me." Like, absolutely determined not to fall into that stupid boy trap, thinking, no way am I planning my free time and weekends and life around these stupid boys. I have spent a great deal of time avoiding these situations, because I see. I see that it's not permanent, that these guys just run around and try to say the right things and do the right things trying to, whatever, make out or cop a feel or get in your pants and all that. And I'm like, Not Me. No way. *Beat.* And then you. You come along and don't push. You're sweet. You're smart. Funny. You can hold a conversation that's not about video games or sports. You notice when I'm wearing something different. When I get my hair cut or wear it a different way. You like, respect me and treat me nice and . . .

She turns away.

God this sounds so stupid!

PETER: No, it doesn't.

GABBY: It's so different than anything I've ever seen from anyone else. I have never seen anyone else get treated the way you have treated me. So, I, whatever, let you in? I let you in. And now . . . now I randomly catch you kissing Tommy Miller in the Chem Lab. *Beat.* So you're gay. Whatever. That's fine. I feel stupid that I was too naïve to catch on before, but okay, whatever. Proms are supposed to be momentous occasions. This has certainly been a momentous occasion.

Beat. She turns to him, direct.

But I have to suspect that you knew about this long before I did. I don't believe that this was some, what, random, freak occurrence.

PETER: . . . No. It wasn't.

GABBY: So what was I to you? Huh? Was I, like, some sort of experiment? Some like, barometer for heterosexuality? A human litmus test?

PETER: No.

GABBY: Then what, Peter? And don't try to hide behind some stupid bullshit excuse because if you do I'll come over there and take that stupid flower off your lapel and stab you in the ear with it.

PETER: I don't know, I can't . . .

GABBY: Because if you were—and I have to believe that you were because you can't seem to even attempt to placate me with some semblance of an excuse—if you were using me as some test, that makes you slime. Because you knew. And you used me. And that makes you worse than any dumb guy, worse than slime. That makes you shit. *Beat.* So look at me. Look at me and promise me that you weren't using me like that.

Silence. She stares at him, then throws her hands up in exasperation.

GABBY: Happy Prom, Peter.

She moves to exit. PETER blocks her. She moves again, he blocks her again.

Will you move, please?

PETER: No. I won't.

GABBY: *Flush.* Why not? You want me to make an even bigger fool of myself? Okay, here goes: I love you. Loved you.

PETER: You don't love me, Gabby.

GABBY:: Don't tell me what I feel!

PETER: You like me. A lot probably. But not love. Like.

GABBY: You have no idea what's in my head. You make me sick.

PETER: I'm sorry.

GABBY: You should be. I want to throw up right now. On you. I feel so stupid! God, I am so stupid!

PETER: You're not stupid.

GABBY: Oh no? You don't think so? Well let's confirm it, then. In addition to having you be the first person—besides immediate family—to say . . . that . . . to, there's more. Tonight? After Prom? I wanted to . . . *Indicates with a shrug.* . . . with you.

PETER: We haven't even kissed.

GABBY: I know that. I thought you were . . . being . . . a gentleman. *Beat.* Whatever, it's so, stupid and corny and traditional and all that, but it's . . . what I wanted.

Beat. Looks at him.

I love you.

PETER: *Softly.* Gabby? You don't love me. You don't. Maybe you wanted to, but . . .

GABBY: Why are you doing this? Stop, just stop . . .

PETER: I think you already justified everything enough for both of us, but, whatever, let's get it out there. You're right, I was the first guy who came along and . . . said the right things . . . complimented you, made you feel pretty and funny and smart, made you feel special . . . made you feel good . . . And I want you to know that I didn't mean to . . . no, wait, that's wrong, I meant to, but I didn't mean to, mean to . . . like, I meant to make you feel good, but I wasn't trying to hurt you, I think is what I mean. No, I know. I mean . . .

GABBY: Stop it.

PETER: Why is it that every time I try to make sense of something I end up making it worse? What the fuck is wrong with me? It's like, like I have this incredible gift for saying the most horribly wrong things at the wrong times.

GABBY: Ya think?

PETER: This isn't going to make much sense . . .

GABBY: None of this has made much sense.

PETER: This isn't going to make much sense to you because this doesn't make much sense to me, but I'm going to say it because if I stop to think about it I might not ever say it. Okay? So just let me talk and then we'll deal with the aftermath.

Takes a breath, begins.

When I was eight, I caught my mom stuffing my Christmas stocking. Caught her red-handed, hand in the stocking, assorted trinkets in her other hand, no room for explanation. So at eight? No Santa—he's dead to me. So I know this—fact—there is no Santa. But even after that, even after I knew, I wanted so badly to believe in Santa that I, what, I tricked myself. For another three years I tricked myself. And now? We're here. But that's not all . . . you ready? Here goes . . . I love you, Gabby. I really do. When we started . . . dating . . . I kept thinking that things would, whatever, change and all that. That I would become attracted to who I am supposed to be attracted to. That didn't happen. And I'm sorry for that. But it doesn't change the fact that I love you, in spite of me, because of, because . . . you are the best person I know. The best.

There's no denying that. You are the best. And I am sorry, Gab. You have no idea how sorry I am that this happened tonight, of all nights. I never would have planned this, you have to understand that, never in a million years, because that would make me slime. It just happened. You have to believe that. *Beat.* But . . .

GABBY: I do . . .

PETER: *Snaps.* Let me finish! Sorry. I told you to let me finish.

GABBY: Sorry.

PETER: As I was saying . . . BUT . . . if there were ever going to be someone, a girl—no, a woman . . . it would . . . be you. And I don't mean that in some sort of, cereal box, consolation prize way, but in a way that's as honest as anything I can ever say. If there was? It would be you. Does that make sense? *Beat. Embarrassed.* Uhhh . . . maybe I should go now. I feel—really—stupid . . .

He moves to exit. GABBY *blocks his path.*

GABBY: Stop it, Peter. Okay? Stop. Don't be a stupid guy.

Short beat. She smirks.

Nice rom-com speech, by the way. Cheesy, but effective.

PETER: Which rom-com?

GABBY: Probably something with Bradley Cooper in it. He's hot.

PETER: He is hot!

She hits him.

Except when he dances with *The Hunger Games* chick. Then not so much.

Laughter. A long beat. Teenage angst.

PETER: So . . .

GABBY: Sew buttons.

PETER: What do we do?

GABBY: We go out there and pretend that this is . . .

PETER: Kiss me.

GABBY: What?

PETER: Kiss me. Please? Kiss me.

GABBY: I don't think so.

PETER: Remember what I said about the consolation prize? I meant that. But there's a very good chance that you may be the last woman I ever kiss. I want you to be the last woman I ever kiss. So . . . kiss me.

GABBY: After you kissed Tommy Miller? I don't think so.

PETER *moves to* GABBY. *She stands her ground. Both of them flush, nervous.* PETER *puts his hands awkwardly on her hips and leans in to kiss her. They bump heads.*

PETER: I'm sorry . . . that was . . .

He turns to retreat. GABBY *grabs his hand, pulls him back to her. She moves his hands to her waist, turns her head, lines herself up, and gently puts her hand on his face, and . . . they kiss.*

END OF PLAY

THE LAST PARTY

Emily Chadick Weiss

The Last Party was originally produced at Death by Audio, Williamsburg Brooklyn, New York, in "A Night of Short Plays" on Thursday, June 23, 2011. Directed by Dylan McCullough.

ORIGINAL CAST
STASIA: Megan Tusing
LENA: Lucy DeVito
HATER: Steven Boyer

CHARACTERS

STASIA: *17, any race. A girl who tries her best to look pretty.*
LENA: *15, any race. A girl who loves looking funky.*
HATER: *17, any race. A disgusting teenaged boy.*

TIME

The present day.

SETTING

The furnished basement of a New York City brownstone, set up for a high school party to happen that evening.

> STASIA *stuffs her face with chocolate cake. Between bites, she is constantly checking her iPhone.* LENA *listens happily on the couch. A few seconds pass as* STASIA *eats, then drinks a bottle of beer. She looks at her phone.*

STASIA: It's eleven thirty.

LENA: Most parties I've been to get really awesome around now.

STASIA: Sarcastic. More awesome than this?

> *She eats.* STASIA *gets a loud text message. She reads it.*

Please stop texting me. It makes me think there will be more than two people at my party.

LENA: Just trying to lighten the mood.

STASIA: Of course everyone's at Jab's party. There's nothing any-one would rather do than spend their last night at Jab's penthouse overlooking all five friggin' boroughs.

LENA: His parties aren't that great. There's just good music.

STASIA: The one party I have. The one time my parents say yes. God, don't people want to try something new?

LENA: People are boring.

STASIA: I'm boring. Everyone else is cool—cool enough not to be here. What was I thinking? Oh I know, I'll suddenly get really popular the last night of my life! What an idiot.

LENA: Stop. Is this the last way you want to feel?

STASIA: You know who I feel like?

LENA: The version of you that's really sorry for yourself?

STASIA: I feel like Hater.

LENA: Eww, why?

STASIA: If he had a party, no one would come. He was the one person I didn't invite.

LENA: Ouch.

STASIA: Would you invite him?

LENA: Hell no, he never brushes his teeth.

STASIA: And he writes all that gross stuff on the boys' bathroom walls. Like "horse cock pussy slime."

LENA: Eww.

STASIA: "Booger finger tuna licker."

LENA: Eww.

STASIA: "Butt crack crumbles seltzer."

LENA: Stop! How do you even know about those?

STASIA: Casey told me. God, I wish he were here.

LENA: I know. You guys would have been cute together.

STASIA: I know . . . Did you know Hater asked me out?

LENA: What? When?

STASIA: Last year.

LENA: What did he say?

STASIA: "You're pretty—be with me Stasia. See you under the scaffolding."

LENA: Eww, what'd you say?

STASIA: I just tried not to breathe in his garbage mouth and walked away.

LENA: Weird.

STASIA: Yeah, you don't exactly get invited to my party that way.

Beat. She checks her phone. She pushes her cake away.

Now I'll just die fat and lonely.

LENA: What about me?

STASIA: I mean fat and with you. But of course you're here, you love me.

LENA: I like your vision.

STASIA: What does that mean?

LENA: I like how you see stuff—like you're ambitious but you're also such a girl. It's great.

STASIA: You're so random.

LENA: I know. A lot of people don't like that about me.

STASIA: A lot of people don't like me at all.

LENA: After the tsunami, there will be no one left to remember how popular you were.

> STASIA *gets sad.*

STASIA: I kind of wish my parents were home.

LENA: They're not upstairs?

STASIA: They went to a key party?

LENA: Weird.

STASIA: Wouldn't you want to spend your last night with your kids?

LENA: You wouldn't want them at your party.

STASIA: They said they wouldn't be home late. Eleven thirty is kind of late for them though.

LENA: Well, it is a key party. Do you know what a key party is?

STASIA: It's like a scavenger hunt, right?

Beat.

LENA: Yeah. *Pause.* I guess we'll both die virgins.

> *The doorbell rings. They both jump.*

Someone came!

> STASIA *fixes her hair and her clothes. She opens the door. It's seventeen-year-old, unattractive, greasy* HATER. *She blocks him from the rest of the room.*

LENA: Hater!

STASIA: What are you doing here?

HATER: I came to party.

STASIA: You weren't invited.

HATER looks around.

HATER: No one's here?

He laughs maniacally.

Good thing I came or else you'd die alone. Hey Lena.

LENA: Why'd you come if you weren't invited?

He pops open a beer, shoves a fistful of cake in his mouth, and washes it down with the beer.

HATER: *With his mouth full.* I have my reasons.

He makes himself comfortable. LENA scoots to the other end of the couch.

STASIA: Please leave. You are the last person I want to see on my last night.

HATER: You're not my first choice either, but the clock is ticking.

LENA: What does that mean?

HATER: It means that tsunami is not drowning me a virgin.

LENA and STASIA exchange a look.

LENA: You think you're getting laid tonight?

HATER: I know I'm getting laid tonight.

STASIA: Not by us.

HATER: I was thinking just you Staszy, but I'll take your sidekick, too.

LENA: I'd kill you before I had sex with you.

HATER: Cute.

He pops some cheese balls into his mouth, then stands up close to STASIA. She backs away.

STASIA: What are you doing?

HATER: Just getting you excited.

STASIA: Go away!

LENA: I'm calling the police.

HATER: You think they're working tonight? They're all at the bars trying to get laid just like me.

He keeps following STASIA.

STASIA: Stop!

> LENA *shoves* HATER *down to the couch. He manages to pin her down. She screams.* STASIA *pulls his hair and kicks him in the back. He yells.*

Get off her.

HATER: We'll both get off.

> *He laughs.* LENA *squirms but can't get up.*

LENA *to* STASIA: Do something!

> STASIA *looks for sharp objects.*

Break the bottle!

> HATER *laughs.*

HATER: This is better than I thought!

> STASIA *kicks him hard in the face.* HATER *groans. She kicks him again. And again.*

Okay!

> *He stands, at the same level as* STASIA *again. This time she doesn't back away.* LENA *manages to get up.*

LENA: Uggh, have you EVER brushed your teeth?

HATER: I don't care for it.

> *He grabs* STASIA*'s waist. She lets him. No resistance.*

STASIA: You want to die knowing you had to force someone to have sex with you?

HATER: I don't care.

STASIA: You wouldn't rather die knowing someone really wanted you?

HATER: I don't care.

STASIA: Because it feels really good when someone wants you.

LENA: Yeah.

HATER: Well no one really wants me, so deal with it.

STASIA: Well then go ahead, have your way with me. I'll die hating you.

HATER: Why aren't you running away?

STASIA: This night can't be saved. Might as well be raped by the most disgusting guy I know before I'm electrocuted by the party lights.

LENA: I can't let you do that.

STASIA: My parents don't care about me, I'm the second-least-liked person in the grade, what else is left.

HATER: Ugh. *Pause.* I don't want to give it up to a sad girl. Let's go Lena.

LENA: I told you I'd kill you before I had sex with you.

He looks at both girls.

HATER: I know you would.

He sits down on the couch, defeated. It's quiet for a moment.

Yeast infection soup!

He punches a pillow.

LENA: Eww.

He takes a breath, then stands.

HATER: I'm going home. Better to die alone in peace than force my way into hearts that have no place for me.

LENA: You didn't want to get into our hearts.

STASIA: His parents are rich; he could have gotten a hooker.

LENA: Don't fall for it; he's just trying something else.

HATER: I'm trying to make a graceful exit. Take care ladies. Hope to see you in heaven.

He walks to the door.

STASIA: Wait.

HATER *turns around.*

I don't want my last feeling to be guilt.

HATER: What do you want it to be?

STASIA: Surprise.

She approaches him and is about to kiss him when LENA *charges* HATER.

LENA: NOOOOO!

She pushes HATER *down to the floor and holds the pillow over his face. He struggles.*

Finally he is still.

LENA: How was that for surprise?

Suddenly, STASIA'*s phone gets a loud text message.* STASIA, *scared, slowly picks it up. She gasps.*

What does it say?

STASIA: The tsunami hit Florida. It skipped New York.

END OF PLAY

LEVITICUS
Bekah Brunstetter

Leviticus was produced as part of *Playground Rules* by Slant Theatre Project. It was directed by Adam Knight and performed by the following cast:

LUCY: Sue Jean Kim
GREG: Scott Kerns

CHARACTERS
LUCY: 17, a good girl.
GREG: 18, a good boy.

TIME
Summer. Late at night.

SETTING
The woods. A warm clearing.

SCENE 1
> *The sound of acoustic music and group singing, far off. LUCY wears a dress. GREG wears shorts. They watch each other hesitantly.*

LUCY: Do you have AIDS or anything?

GREG: What?

LUCY: Do you?

GREG: No . . .

LUCY: I guess I'm gonna take my clothes off, but don't look at me.

GREG: Like all of them?

LUCY: I guess I don't have to.

GREG: Not like all of them. Just—not that it—I mean, I'm extremely comfortable with my body. So. And and and yours.

> *Beat.*

LUCY: You should kiss me for a minute.

> *He kisses her sweetly. Then:*

I'm a virgin.

GREG: I'm a virgin.

> *Beat.*

LUCY: . . . You're a virgin?

GREG: Um—no—I mean no . . .

LUCY: You're a VIRGIN!

GREG: Your mom's a virgin.

> *Beat.*

LUCY: What?

GREG: Anyways, so, yeah.

LUCY: Are you seriously a virgin?

GREG: Ha—um . . . I mean, yeah, I've had a lot of—sure, but—I've never—completely—sealed the—sailed the—all of the. Way. Up in it. So.

Beat.

LUCY: Well, then is this really—the right—?

Beat.

GREG: Oh—Oh, definitely. Lucy, listen to me, I mean, yeah. I mean, I really like you. And we've been together for almost two weeks, so . . .

LUCY: Yeah—it's not exactly like we're rushing or anything . . .

GREG: Plus camp's almost over. Plus I just . . .

LUCY: What?

GREG: I just WANT to—I just really freaking want to—do you?

LUCY: Yeah—I mean YEAH . . .

GREG: I'm tired of everyone telling me no and telling me not to, F that. F rules that don't make any sense to me.

LUCY: *A confession.* Sometimes I smoke cigarettes and I pretty much covet constantly. I feel like all I do all day is covet so hard.

GREG: I don't wanna wait anymore.

LUCY:: I feel like I've been waiting since I was born.

GREG: It's—it's like Europe, I think.

LUCY: Yeah, Europe . . .

GREG: Who cares if it's scary or far away, you just gotta go there, it's part of being alive, you have a responsibility as a human BE-ING, as one of God's kids, to see the Earth . . .

LUCY: Oh my God—it's exactly like Europe . . .

GREG: You just gotta GO there!

They make out. GREG, extremely tentatively, begins to put a hand up her dress. LUCY stops him, jerking it away.

LUCY: Wow—wow . . .

GREG: Sorry . . .

LUCY: Wow—just hold on—can we . . .

GREG: Sure, sure . . .

> LUCY *sits.* GREG *sits next to her. Beat.*

LUCY: You can kiss me again if you want.

GREG: Oh—um, okay . . .

LUCY: But how are we supposed to—um—can you tell what you're going to do before you do it—just so that I know—is that okay?

GREG: Before I do it? What if I'm not sure?

LUCY: Or while you're doing it . . .

GREG: Like a doctor?

LUCY: Yeah . . .

GREG: I'm putting my hand on your knee.

> *He does so.*

LUCY: Okay . . .

GREG: I'm—well I'm about to, I think—I'm going to move my hand—up your—into—your . . .

LUCY: *Quickly, stopping him.* Let's just breathe for a minute.

> *Beat. They breathe.*

GREG: Did you ever play Doctor when you were little?

LUCY: No, did you?

GREG: Um, constantly. You really didn't?

LUCY: No, is that weird?

GREG: You missed out, a lot. Man, was it informative.

> *Beat. He looks at her. She's tense.*

You gotta relax.

LUCY: I was molested.

GREG: What? Really?

LUCY: No.

GREG: Did you used to—ever—when you were little?

LUCY: What?

GREG: Touch—um—touch . . .

LUCY: *Quickly.* Of course I did.

GREG: If you said you didn't, I woulda called you a liar. Everyone who says they never have lies like a dog. It's so weird, when you're little. When you don't get it but it seems like such a big freaking deal.

LUCY: It is, it is a big freaking deal—it's the biggest freaking deal pretty much ever. 'Cause once you, once you go to Europe, you can't go back. You can't un-go.

GREG: Yeah, but then you've been to Europe. *Beat.* I used to hump my teddy bear.

LUCY: *Laughing.* What?

GREG: Yeah—like every night. Not like—to the point where I actually—um—but . . . And then one night I dreamt the teddy bear came to life and murdered me.

LUCY: How?

GREG: Slit my throat.

LUCY: And then what?

GREG: I stopped humping my teddy bear.

Beat. A cold breeze.

LUCY: I guess the thing is—I used to—dream—or daydream or something—that—s—sex was—it was—this was before I got it, before I knew what it actually, yeah. I used to think that you go to this—place—to have It. To do It. And you don't want to go but you have to. You get Sent. And if you're a girl, they tie you to a table. Like an operating table. Not tie, bind. Metal handcuffs that come up around your limbs and keep you there. And you're naked and cold and you don't want it but you have to. And then there's this scientist person making sure you're strapped in tight. Then they leave the room but they're watching through a little window in the door like a dentist taking an x-ray. And if you're the girl, you're laying there and the room goes dim. And there's a metal sound from above you. And then the boy descends. He's strapped to the ceiling and the ceiling is coming down on top of you. He's being lowered on top of you. And you're squirming and you don't want it but you're stuck and the scientist is watching through the window and then the boy is on top of you and he's kissing you and you don't want it and he's inside of you and it hurts but you can't do anything about it. Then suddenly, or slowly, you start to like it. You can't help it. You realize you want it and this happens pretty quickly like a hot wave of like a wanting and just when you are going to die from wanting to move, the scientist knows that exact moment and from outside the room, he pushes a button, and you are released. The cuffs are gone. The boy is released and you reach for each other and claw at each other and you just do it and do it and do it and then it's done. And when it's done, the boy is lifted up. You don't even get to say bye. And you are bound again, and then another boy comes and it starts all over again and you're cold and scared. And you look to the window at the scientist and that's when you realize or guess that it's not a scientist, it's God or Jesus and he winks at you and it happens all over again. *Beat.* I'm worried I have—issues . . .

GREG: Um . . .

LUCY: Like I'm going to—like I'll always have issues . . .

> *GREG doesn't know what to say. The far-away song turns to a capella. Lucy starts to cry.*

GREG: Are you—um . . .

LUCY: I'm sorry. I'm sorry. Did you hear that? They went a capella. A capella music makes me cry.

GREG: Why?

LUCY: 'Cause it's so naked . . .

> *He kisses her. She lets it happen. It escalates.*

GREG: I'm going to do it . . .

> *Lights go down.*

SCENE 2

> *Lights back up. Post It. GREG and LUCY are a bit disheveled, but nothing has changed. They sit, both looking a bit disappointed. LUCY looks up.*

LUCY: Trees are pretty.

GREG: Yeah, so is the sky.

> *Beat.*

LUCY: I don't feel any / different.

GREG: Neither do I.

> *Beat.*

I guess we should get back.

LUCY: Yeah, I guess.

> *But neither move.*

This is the last summer. After this summer, we'll never have to go to church camp ever again.

GREG: Until we have kids and make them go.

LUCY: Take them shopping first for socks and lollipops.

GREG: And then we'll have to drive them here and drop them off at the entrance and our hands will turn wet from the memories and we'll drive off so fast we'll plow through kids and their families walking towards the bunks.

LUCY: They'll make us bookmarks out of leaves with verses from First Corinthians.

GREG: And they won't know why they're here.

LUCY: And we won't tell them.

GREG: But they'll learn all the songs at least.

LUCY: I love the songs.

GREG: They'll come home singing them.

LUCY: And they'll come home singing them and I'll cry into their sandwiches.

GREG: And they won't know why we sent them here.

LUCY: And we won't tell them.

> *A beat.* LUCY *sneezes.*

GREG: God bless you.

LUCY: Thank you.

> *A beat. They sit. Lights go out.*

END OF PLAY

LOCKDOWN WITH PINKY

C.S. Hanson

CHARACTERS

BIRDIE COMBS: *18, female. She is dressed in jeans and a shirt.*

PINKY WALKER: *18, male. He is chunky and is dressed up for Halloween as a glamor girl in a tight dress, stiletto heels, and plenty of dangling jewelry.*

TIME

The present.

SETTING

A room in a nursing home with minimal furnishings.

> BIRDIE *and* PINKY *are alone in a sparsely furnished room. The front door has just slammed shut.*

BIRDIE: Is she going to be—? She's not gonna . . . ?

PINKY: Die?

BIRDIE: Don't say that. I never meant to . . .

PINKY: I saw it. I saw it with my own eyes.

> BIRDIE *tries to open the door, but it is locked.*

BIRDIE: She was still breathing, wasn't she? Let me outta here. I need to see her.

PINKY: Can't see her now. She's out for observation.

BIRDIE: What's with the door? Why doesn't it . . .

PINKY: This is the Alzheimer's Unit. When that door locks, there's no getting out from in here.

BIRDIE: Call someone. Please. Call someone.

PINKY: I got my orders: "Keep her here 'til the cops come."

BIRDIE: All I was doing was . . . giving her a neck massage.

PINKY: I seen what I seen, and now I need to commit it to memory.

BIRDIE: Commit what to memory? My grandma is crazy. That's why she said what she said.

PINKY: Save it for the police. Here. Stay busy.

> PINKY *tries to give* BIRDIE *a stack of magazines—*People, Entertainment Weekly, Star, *etcetera—but* BIRDIE *doesn't take them.* BIRDIE *pulls her wallet out of her bag.*

BIRDIE: I got twenty-five, six, seven—twenty-seven buck. Let me out, and all this cash is yours.

PINKY: What don't you understand about lockdown? That door is made to lock people in. Gotta lock the patients in their rooms. Else they'll be walking out on the streets, on the railroad tracks, all hours of the day and night.

BIRDIE: Geez.

She takes a bottle out of her handbag and takes a swig.

PINKY: What's that?

BIRDIE: Kool-Aid. . . . What? Might as well. I'm as good as in jail.

PINKY: Doesn't work that way, honey. First I gotta testify. Before that, they gotta read you your *Miranda* rights. I'm gonna make sure they do, too. I watch my *Law and Order*. If they don't read those rights, you might go free and I'll miss my chance to go on the witness stand.

BIRDIE: Your chance? Like you've been waiting for something like this to happen so you can . . .

PINKY: I never said. Just that, I'm familiar with the proceedings. I watch all the cop shows. When I'm not working, I sometimes watch for ten hours in a row: *CSI, Criminal Minds, Breaking Bad, NCIS, NCIS-Los Angeles, Bones, The Mentalist,* reruns of *Law and* . . .

BIRDIE: You think anyone will believe anything you have to say? Look at you.

PINKY: This is my Halloween costume. Where's yours? *Pause.* Couldn't think of nothing? I say to myself every day, "Pinky Walker, invent something new." And I do, every day. Last week, I experimented with lip gloss. You know you can mix them together right on your lips? Mmmm. For Halloween, I'm not just a regular glamor girl, I'm glamor girl to the extreme.

BIRDIE: Glad I didn't dress up. At this rate, won't make it to the party anyway.

PINKY: You got invited to a Halloween party?

BIRDIE: Haven't been to a party in, like, two years. What does it matter? I'm going to jail, because you got this idea life is like a *Law and Order* episode—which it isn't.

PINKY: Let the facts stand for themselves, honey. I am the only witness. I saw you trying to strangle that sweet old lady to death. To death.

BIRDIE: She's not sweet. She's never been sweet. So don't call her sweet.

PINKY: Don't matter. You're the prime suspect. They gonna take you in a room and there'll be two cops—good cop and bad cop. And one of them is gonna bang on the desk and rough you up, while the other says sweet things in your ear and pretty soon you'll be crying and grinding your teeth up and writing every detail on a piece of paper. And, if there are things you don't remember? No problem, girlfriend. I have now committed to memory everything I saw, and I can even demonstrate how you did it if called upon to do so.

> *He mimics with his hands the act of strangling someone around the neck.*

BIRDIE: Some people should be dead. Don't you think? *Pause.* You work here. Don't you ever think so?

PINKY: I am a health-care professional.

BIRDIE: Professional? You're an aide. You're one step up from janitor.

PINKY: Oh, girlfriend, you make me wanna slap your face, but I am on duty as a health-care professional and I am going to keep my hands at my side.

BIRDIE: Slap me. The police will like that part of the story.

PINKY: They know me. From when I worked over in assisted living. The demented people was always escaping and the cops would round 'em up. I was a star witness as to the direction they might have gone. Since I got promoted to the Alzheimer's Unit, I don't see them as much. But they remember me. 'Cause I got style. Everywhere I go. Pinky Walker has a certain style. Never met a shade of lipstick that didn't look good on me. I make old men smile like sweethearts. Old ladies admire me for my sophistication. It's important for the job. Keeps us all alive.

BIRDIE: What's the good of being alive if you're out of your head? If you have to be locked up so you don't go walking out, getting run over?

PINKY: Your grandma's not every minute out of her head. We discuss the news.

BIRDIE: *Referring to the magazines.* You call that news?

PINKY: Stop talking. I'm not listening to an attempted murderer in the first degree. I gotta keep my memories intact.

BIRDIE: Grandma used to put brandy in my hot cocoa. That's a good memory.

PINKY: I'm sure your cell mates will be very interested.

BIRDIE: Once grandma and I were in rehab at the same time. She got a new hip and I, well, I was in a different kind of facility.

PINKY: None of this is news to me. I know you're in trouble with the law, Birdie.

BIRDIE: You don't know nothing about me or my family.

PINKY: I do so. They gave you that name 'cause you chirped like a bird instead of cried like a baby. Ha. What a name you got, Birdie. They shoulda named you after a wild animal. I bet you got expelled more times than me. You ever learn to cry, Birdie? Not quite human if you didn't.

BIRDIE: If I'm so inhuman, maybe I should go all the way and kill you, too.

PINKY: Police gonna be here. I think I hear a siren. You got no time for another killing.

BIRDIE: There's no siren. They won't waste the siren on me. I been in the backseat of a police car before. I been in handcuffs. The more you twist, the tighter they get. Kind of like strangling someone around the neck. Crack, done, dead. I should have been quicker. I'd like to do it again.

PINKY: Again? There. You admitted it. You're guilty.

BIRDIE:: I might as well go for broke. Come here.

PINKY: Don't kill me. You can take my new alligator bag if you want. It's in my locker. I'll get it when they open the door.

BIRDIE: Is it as fake as those long fingernails of yours?

PINKY: Keep your hands off me. The judge is gonna hear about this.

BIRDIE: If I go to jail, who's gonna visit her? Not my mom. Not the other relatives. Everyone's so busy, right? No one likes the

Alzheimer's Unit. Know what they say? "She won't remember anyway."

PINKY: Don't try to soften me up. Murder is big. Maybe they'll call the DA. That's "district attorney," honey. And some investigators for sure.

BIRDIE: You don't know what you're talking about. If dispatch got a hold of this, my PO will get here before the rest.

PINKY: PO?

BIRDIE: Told you it's not like on TV. Probation officer. He put me on a three-year plan. I promised to follow it so I don't have to go to jail. My PO, get this, told the judge that I am a person of good character. Two years now, going to meetings, staying clean. I'm so clean I don't even have to shower. Now you're gonna ruin all that?

PINKY: This PO guy? He can keep you outta jail after you strangled your own grandma?

BIRDIE: No, Pinky. He probably can't. I'll get hauled in. Busted. For what good? All because you wanna live out your dream of being on that witness stand?

PINKY: Some people just get crazy on Halloween. But that's no excuse for murder.

BIRDIE: Halloween's got nothing to do with it. Sometimes when I see her I can almost taste the hot cocoa and that gets me to craving the brandy. But no, that's not why you saw me doing, you know. I just plain can't stand her being out of her mind. Today, she yells at me, "Why'd you have to drive with the baby in your lap? You shouldn't be driving with the baby in your lap."

PINKY: She remembered the baby?

BIRDIE: I don't have a baby. I could have had three babies by now but God knows I didn't let . . .

PINKY: She was thinking you were Britney.

BIRDIE: And then she looks right at me and calls me a bitch.

PINKY: Well now that is something.

BIRDIE: I come here every week to visit her and she calls me a—? I mean, it's just, I didn't need that. Don't go to parties anymore. Go to school every day. And after that I'm working cash register in the grocery store. Counting change for tight asses who, I love this, who throw those dumb magazines in their cart at the last minute, sorta cover 'em up, like they're too good to read *National Enquirer*. Everybody reads crap. You know how I get my kicks? I squeeze lemons and make the sourest lemonade I can, so sour it's hard to drink. But I drink it. And I put Tabasco sauce in my coffee. Never see my old friends any more. There's so much I . . . avoid. And she calls me a bitch?

PINKY: Maybe it wasn't like "bitch" bitch. Maybe it was warmly bitch.

BIRDIE: I think you're the bitch. You're the high-maintenance bitch. With your nails and painted face and hair and tight-ass way you dress. I used to dress like you. Dress like I was having fun. Not anymore.

PINKY: Something you need to understand: When Britney put her baby in her lap and drove the SUV, you remember that?

BIRDIE: Who?

PINKY: Long time ago. Britney Spears. She drove with her baby in her lap, she mighta been drunk and I don't think she buckled up, and she got arrested.

BIRDIE: So?

PINKY: Your grandma loved that story. She made me read it over and over. And every time, she'd say, "I love that bitch." And I just went with it and pretty soon we was calling each other bitch. "Good morning, bitch! How ya doing, sweetie bitch? You gonna be okay, bitch? Okay, I see you tomorrow, bitch." Kinda means "I love you."

BIRDIE: But you saw me. And my grandma knows I tried to . . . She's probably gone by now. Like, dead gone.

PINKY: No way. She's kicking ass. And tomorrow she'll be pissing and pooping on the floor. And I'll be cleaning up and I'll give her a big smile and go to her, "How's my darling bitch, huh, how you doing?"

BIRDIE: Take care of her when I can't be here, okay?

PINKY: What you talking about?

BIRDIE: I'm going to jail.

PINKY: I, uh, I just giving you a hard time 'cuz you still in school and you got a lot going for you. I dropped out, so I gotta make the most of this, see? You got a Halloween party to go to.

BIRDIE: The cops are coming for me. I know how this works. The party? It's just the grocery store people. Not a big deal.

PINKY: Look, crazy people always accusing people of murder. Most people who come in here to visit, you can tell, they just wanna strangle their relations and put them out of their misery. Out of everyone's misery. But then, I'd be out of a job if that happened. Girlfriend, you's the first time we got close to a real murder. Hey, look at that, my shift is over. What time's the party?

BIRDIE: My grandma is going to be talking about this. If I confess, at least she won't seem crazier than she already is.

PINKY: She don't remember what she ate for breakfast. She's not gonna remember a little neck massage. Her memories, they're from long ago. She goes on and on about screwing a governor and getting shut-up money to keep quiet. Wouldn't be surprised if he's your grandpa. And she has a keen memory for Britney Spears. Don't ask me why.

BIRDIE: What are you saying? Can I leave?

PINKY: Girlfriend, I shop at your store on a regular basis. I would give anything to go to that Halloween party. I'll take care of the police. You think any of those boys who work behind the counter slicing up meat gonna be at the party? Got my eye on one of them.

BIRDIE: I don't have a costume.

PINKY: Oh yes you do. Birdie Combs, you're going as The Girl Who Tried to Strangle Her Grandma.

BIRDIE: *Smiling.* Okay, bitch.

END OF PLAY

MANDALA

John J. Kelly

Mandala was performed as an in-school workshop at Atlantic High School in Port Orange, Florida, in November of 2012 under the direction of Mickey Griffiths. The play premiered on May 4, 2013, at Elmira College in Elmira, New York, under the direction of Margaret Reed, with the following cast:

KATHERINE: Sarah Adriance
FIONA: Ali Hutchinson
ANNA: Madelaine Whalen
THERESA: J. C. Trichanh

CHARACTERS
KATHERINE: *about 16, a girl.*
THERESA: *about 17, a girl of Asian heritage.*
ANNA: *about 17, a girl of Native American heritage.*
FIONA: *about 17, a girl.*

TIME
The present.

SETTING
A room in the YWCA.

NOTE: A mandala is a Tibetan sand painting, similar to the sand paint-ings of the Navajo people. The Tibetan work is elaborate, with the exact balance of the work symbolizing balance in existence. The actual man-dala called for in the script can be simpler, with large regions within the circumference of the work filled quite simply prior to the performance. A search of the web will provide many examples of both Tibetan mandalas and Navajo sand paintings.

> *A small room in a local YWCA. A large folding table stands upstage, against the wall. A pizza delivery box with remnants of a pizza sit on the table, as does some soft drinks and cups. In the cen-ter of the room stands a cube with a square board on top. An almost finished mandala sits on the board. A number of small children's chairs are available, some surrounding the cube. At curtain rise the girls are working on the mandala.*

KATHERINE: *Stops working.* Is this okay? What do you think?

THERESA: It's fine.

ANNA: It looks great. But that's not the point.

KATHERINE: It is to me.

ANNA: It's the sharing, the experience . . .

KATHERINE: They died! The least we can do is get it perfect.

THERESA: *Still working.* And what is "perfect"?

> *She stops working.*

What will make it perfect?

KATHERINE: I don't know. I just know I want it that way.

Crosses to table.

ANNA: *Crossing to her.* I'm sorry. I didn't mean . . .

KATHERINE: Why are you even here? Maura and Sue were our friends. You barely knew them.

ANNA: I knew them.

KATHERINE: Not like we did. Not like us!

ANNA: No.

KATHERINE: So why are doing this?

THERESA: Why shouldn't she?

KATHERINE: What?

THERESA: Why shouldn't she? The mandala is for everyone. It's communal.

ANNA: *After a pause, softly.* It's what we do.

THERESA: Why don't we get back to it?

FIONA: *Entering.* Finally! I tried calling your cell, Terri—yours too, Kath. They just kept going to voice mail. I finally had to call your mom. She told me you were here.

THERESA: We've been here all weekend, working. Ever since . . .

FIONA: Why didn't you call me? Do you know what it's been like?

THERESA: Yes, we do.

She crosses to and hugs FIONA.

KATHERINE: *Joining the hug.* And we did try to call you—several times—but your phone was always busy.

FIONA: I still can't believe it. Three days ago we went to the mall with them. Now, all of a sudden, they're gone.

She notices ANNA.

ANNA: Hi, I'm Anna.

FIONA: Fiona.

KATHERINE: *To Fiona.* Anna's from Riverside. She worked with Maura at Caroline's on weekends.

To ANNA:

Fiona goes to Southport with us.

FIONA: Hi.

To the others.

I had to talk to someone, you know? I tried my mom, but she didn't know what to say, and my dad just wanted to fix everything. To make it better.

THERESA: It's hard on them, too.

FIONA: I guess.

THERESA: Listen, we're sorry. We should have tried to call you again. We meant to, but once we got started, we sort of got involved.

FIONA: *Crossing to the mandala.* So, what is it?

KATHERINE: *As all cross downstage.* It's a mandala.

FIONA: A mandala?

THERESA: A symbol . . . a physical—I don't know, representation—of our thoughts and feelings. It's a way of remembering. Honoring. And it's something to do. We couldn't just sit around and do nothing.

FIONA: *Nods yes, then asks:* Asian?

THERESA: Tibetan. Ancient. Part of Buddhist and Hindu rituals, but it's probably much older. It means "circle" in Sanskrit.

ANNA: It's a part of my culture as well. Native American. We've been using sand paintings since the beginning.

FIONA: Really? How come I've never heard of them?

ANNA: Lots of people know about them. Lots don't.

THERESA: The circle symbolizes wholeness. It's a reminder of our relation to the infinite. The Aztec calendar is thought to come from it, the labyrinth and the Indian medicine wheel as well.

ANNA: The dream-catcher. The Navajo believe it to symbolize the impermanence of life.

KATHERINE: That certainly applies.

FIONA: So . . . can I join you?

THERESA: It wouldn't seem right if you didn't.

All but KATHERINE *get back to work.*

KATHERINE: Maybe I should leave you to it? You all were friends,

I just . . .

ANNA: You were just a newer friend—a different friend, in a different way. But you care—cared—and you should be a part.

They all work on the mandala.

FIONA: *After a while.* I just can't believe it. Dead. Because of some stupid accident.

KATHERINE: We all knew about it. Maura just wouldn't stop. She'd text anytime, anywhere. At the movies, during meals . . .

ANNA: At work.

KATHERINE: She almost got us killed driving home from the mall last week.

THERESA: And this week it got her—and Sue—killed. On a stupid trip to buy ice cream.

They all stop, unsure what to do next.

FIONA: So . . . what do we do? What are the rules?

THERESA: Just do what you feel.

FIONA: But I don't want to ruin it.

KATHERINE: I know what you mean. It's sort of religious and, well, I was so worried I'd do something wrong.

ANNA: But there is no wrong—or right, for that matter.

THERESA: A mandala can be many things. It can be about life . . . moments . . . feelings even. It symbolizes everything we are thinking or feeling, but without specific symbols. The symbols are ours, as we feel them, as we see them. What seems right to you is right.

FIONA: But there are four of us. Won't our symbols conflict?

THERESA: Everything in life is in the mandala. Don't worry about it.

FIONA: But how can we all do what's right? Right for whom?

ANNA: When it's right you'll know. We'll all know.

FIONA: *Unsure.* Okay.

They all get to work. After a bit:

KATHERINE: I don't know about you, but I'm hungry. Starved, actually.

Crossing to the pizza.

Anyone else care for some delicious cold pizza?

She eats.

THERESA/ANNA: No. No thanks.

FIONA: I'm not hungry, but I could go for something to drink.

Gets up.

KATHERINE: One cheap, store brand Diet Coke coming up.

She pours a cup.

FIONA: Thanks.

She drinks.

KATHERINE: Wasn't there something, somebody, in psych that used mandalas too? One of the big names?

ANNA: Probably.

KATHERINE: Guess I should have paid more attention in class . . . something about order, psychic order. Getting things back as they should be.

FIONA: You think that's going to happen?

KATHERINE: I don't know. Maybe. Right now I only know I keep seeing Sue, smiling at me. That smile she smiled that first day of kindergarten . . . when she soloed on that silly clarinet . . . when she was ready for her first real date with Tommy Wanamaker.

ANNA: Maura was always running—in high gear—like she was going to miss something if she just walked through life. I don't think I ever saw her doing anything slowly, easily. She rushed through school to get to work. She rushed through work to get home. She rushed getting ready to go out.

FIONA: And her rushing to answer her text got them both killed. Idiot.

KATHERINE: *After a pause.* I guess psychic order is out. Should we just get back to work?

FIONA: Fine.

They all get back to work.

ANNA: I think I've only got a little more to do.

THERESA: We need to clean up the edging as well. If the center of the mandala is supposed to symbolize the essence of our thoughts and feelings, the circumference symbolizes our grasping for that essence, that order you were talking about.

FIONA: And then what? What happens when we're finished?

THERESA: Tradition has it that we take all the sand, collect it, and place it in some moving river where it can be returned to the universe, become part of the whole.

ANNA: It's one final symbolic blessing. Kind of the circle of life.

FIONA: I like that. So let's get it finished.

THERESA: For Maura and Sue.

FIONA: For Maura and Sue?

THERESA: Sure. Why?

FIONA: I'm not doing anything for Maura. It's because of her that Sue is dead.

KATHERINE: But Maura died too.

FIONA: But that was her doing. Sue didn't deserve to die.

THERESA: Nobody deserves to die.

FIONA: Sue died because of her. Her and her stupid . . .

ANNA: *Comforting her.* Yeah . . . we know. Maura. But she deserves this too.

FIONA: Why? Why does she deserve this? What good is this lousy thing anyway?

THERESA: The Chinese would say it would help "become one with the Tao."

FIONA: We're not in China, Terri.

ANNA: Okay. So what do you want to do?

FIONA: Do?

ANNA: Yeah, do. We've been working on this for days. It's our—I don't know, gift?

To both Sue and Maura.

FIONA: But it's Maura's fault.

KATHERINE: So what?

FIONA: *Violently raking once through the mandala with her hand.* So I won't have anything to do with anything for Maura. It's her fault

Sue is dead.

> FIONA *moves away. Everyone is frozen, unsure what has happened, unsure what to do.*

FIONA: *Finally turning back.* I'm sorry.

ANNA: *Angrily.* Are you?

FIONA: Yes. I'm sorry. Sorry that I ruined your work. Sorry that Sue is dead, that I'll never see her again. Sorry that I don't know how to deal with this. With you. Sorry I don't understand my feelings.

KATHERINE: None of knows how to deal with this. We're doing the best we can.

THERESA: It's our way of dealing . . . of coping.

FIONA: I'm sorry. And I'm sorry that Maura is dead.

THERESA: Look . . .

ANNA: *Stopping* THERESA. You're right. It was Maura's fault. Maura's responsibility. And all of us feel an indescribable anger towards her. Her insistent, ridiculous fixation caused their deaths. How can we be anything but mad at her?

FIONA: I'm . . .

ANNA: But she died too. Maura, our good friend, is gone. We've all lost her. She'll never have the life she should have had. She'll never again bring smiles to all our faces. Never marry. Never have children, a husband.

FIONA: Sue and I were going to room together at college. We had it all planned. "Going to State."

> *Overcome, momentarily no one speaks.*

KATHERINE: *Looking at the mandala.* So what do we do with this?

FIONA: I'm so sorry.

ANNA: It's okay.

> *She comforts* FIONA *who is now crying.*

KATHERINE: I guess we can fix it.

> *Starts to fix the mandala.*

It'll just . . .

THERESA: *Stopping her.* No.

KATHERINE: No? But it's . . .

THERESA: It is what it is. What it should be. A symbol of all of our thoughts and feelings. All . . .

FIONA: I don't understand.

THERESA:: The circle of the mandala symbolizes wholeness. The mandala as it now stands symbolizes the wholeness of all our lives, thoughts, and feelings for Sue, and Maura, and ourselves. It's finished. Do you think anything can be added to make it "better?"

To KATHERINE*:*

You wanted it to be perfect. Is it?

KATHERINE: As perfect as we are. As we can be.

THERESA: Then it's time to collect the sands.

She goes to table, gets a bowl, gives it to ANNA.

ANNA: To share them with the whole that is the universe.

Gives the bowl to FIONA.

FIONA: But I just ruined it.

ANNA: No, you completed it. You added what none of us had been able to express.

THERESA: C'mon, let's get going.

They begin collecting sand.

FIONA: You're sure?

KATHERINE: If the center of the mandala is the essence of life, and the circumference the grasping for that essence, we did exactly what we set out to do. Shared Sue, shared Maura, shared of ourselves. And it certainly symbolized the impermanence of life, like you said Anna.

ANNA: So now the only thing to do is to finish it—to return the sands to the running water as a blessing.

THERESA: For Sue, for Maura, for us all.

ANNA: Fiona, was there a place, near the water, where Sue liked to go?

FIONA: The park, just beyond the boat ramp. We used to go there to think, to plan.

ANNA: How about returning the sands there?

FIONA: She'd like that, thanks.

THERESA: Fine with me.

KATHERINE: Is there any special way to do it?

THERESA: Haven't you figured it out by now? You do it as you feel you should. That's all that really matters.   Now c'mon, let's go!

They all begin to exit with the sand.

END OF PLAY

THE OTHER SIDE

Merridith Allen

CHARACTERS

PAIGE: *16; female; an out-of-body spirit.*
CONNER: *16; male; a grim reaper.*

TIME

The present.

SETTING

The hallway of a hospital. And between one world and another.

> *A bare hallway with a closed door upstage. This door leads to a hospital room we will not see. Dim lights. Then, a blackout, followed by an intense flash of white light. Two characters appear, seemingly from thin air. One, PAIGE, stands in front of the door, her arms stretched out, as if she is a human shield. The other, CONNER, wears a black grim reaper's robe and carries a scythe. He grabs PAIGE, trying to yank her from her position.*

CONNER: Move!

PAIGE: No!

CONNER: Paige!

PAIGE: Get off!

CONNER: I'm not kidding!

PAIGE: Me neither!

CONNER: Last warning. They told me to use this . . .

PAIGE: You wouldn't dare . . .

CONNER: Would too—this is that major—I will totally scythe you . . .

PAIGE: You never even had the guts to dissect a worm . . .

CONNER: You don't understand . . .

PAIGE: Yes, I do! I won't let you take her, Conner.

CONNER: You can't stand there forever. Someone's coming for you too—

PAIGE: No, I'm not listening.

> *She covers her ears.*

La, la, la la . . .

CONNER: She's not gonna wake up!

PAIGE: Just because you gave up doesn't mean she will. She could wake up, and so could I . . .

CONNER: You have to move, Paige. For serious.

He lifts the scythe.

I'm gonna count to three. Okay? One . . .

PAIGE: Give her time, Conner . . .

CONNER: Two . . .

PAIGE: Please? For me?

CONNER: *Hesitating.* Two and a half . . .

PAIGE: This is us—Paige, Conner, and Dana—the three musketeers— we held hands at kindergarten graduation—come on, Conner!

CONNER: *Hesitating.* Two and three quarters . . .

She doesn't move.

Okay! You better move.

She doesn't.

I'm gonna do it.

She stares at him.

For real.

She braces.

I warned you. Three!

He torques back to swing. She turns away. He swings. At the very last second, she ducks and rolls away. He swung so hard, his body wrenches and he stumbles, dropping the scythe.

Damn! That's heavy . . .

PAIGE: *Dusting herself off.* I can't believe you did that, you jerk!

CONNER: Oh crap . . . I'm sorry.

He stands.

Not that—I mean I couldn't like, really hurt you, right?

He steps towards her, she retreats.

But . . . you know, you just—you put on that robe, they put this big thing in your hands and, like, okay yeah, I totally got carried away . . .

PAIGE: That's it. Now I'm really not moving.

She plants herself in a guarding position in front of the door again.

CONNER: Aww, come on . . .

PAIGE: No, you come on! Why can't you give her a chance?

CONNER: Believe me, I wish I could, but trust me, there's nothing I can do. I was a goner, like, Bam! Like, on impact. And Dana? She's hangin' on but . . . look, she's next on my list, okay? It's like, done. Here, I'll show you.

He pulls out an iPad.

PAIGE: What the hell—you have a list of dying people on an iPad?

CONNER: Well, yeah—I mean that's why They chose me. Their whole system runs on Mac devices now, so when they need a new Reaper, they're more likely to take a teenager over a—okay, anyway, that's beside the point . . .

PAIGE: Are you sure? Like, really sure it can't be changed, or maybe—I don't know, can we talk to someone? Maybe they made a mistake.

CONNER: They didn't. The big Genius Bar in the sky doesn't have an error margin.

A moment. PAIGE *crosses her arms.*

Don't you remember how bad it was?

PAIGE: Um . . . I don't know . . .

CONNER: Wow. I guess that's the difference between dead and almost dead. I remember everything.

PAIGE: So . . . how bad was it?

CONNER: Let's just say, *The Fast and The Furious* except ten times worse and way less cool looking.

PAIGE: We hit a . . . was it another car?

CONNER: A truck. On the side of the highway. I—well, me and Dana, we were both in the front when . . . well, it took almost the whole top off the car and . . .

PAIGE: Oh, God . . . yeah . . . and I was . . . I had a headache . . .

CONNER: So you asked me to drive us. You were laying down in the back seat. It's all my fault, I wanted to get us to the party faster, and there was that slow-ass dude from like, Florida in front of us, and I just wanted to pass him, right? But it was foggy and . . . I totally fucked up, Paige.

PAIGE: So this is . . .

His iPhone beeps. He checks it.

CONNER: Oh, man. That's a text from my boss. I really do need to go get Dana. If I don't, she'll get stuck, and I'll get in some deep shit then, and . . .

PAIGE: What do you mean, "stuck?"

CONNER: Um, like a ghost, I guess? I haven't gone through the whole Welcome Packet yet, so I don't know exactly, but it's not good. You don't want that for her, do you?

PAIGE: No . . . Conner? Have you seen the other side, like, where we're going?

CONNER: Yeah . . . for a little while, before they sent me for Dana. I'm not supposed to talk about it, but actually, the place looked pretty cool, and things felt good there. Like everyone you know and love is okay and, everything is taken care of.

PAIGE: Sounds nice. You think, um—can I go with you guys? Since we all go together everywhere anyway . . .

CONNER: I asked about that, but you're not on my list, so that means someone else is coming for you, I think.

PAIGE: Like who? My grandma?

CONNER: I don't know.

PAIGE: Can you check?

CONNER: Uh, sure. One sec.

He presses a button.

I just gotta let gCloud synch.

PAIGE: gCloud?

CONNER: Like iCloud, except, you know.

He points up towards heaven. A few moments, then he stares at her.

PAIGE: What? Am I—is it bad? Am I going—is it somewhere bad, what?

CONNER: No. You're . . .

He checks again.

. . . you're not on anybody's list. Let me put in a search real quick.

He does.

Oh, wow. Your name's not anywhere.

PAIGE: What does that mean?

CONNER: That means . . . Paige, I think you're going to be okay.

PAIGE: Oh my God . . .

CONNER: Yeah. That's awesome . . .

PAIGE: But that means . . .

His phone beeps again.

CONNER: Shit. I gotta get Dana. And . . . you gotta let us go. *A pause.* Please, Paige.

She finally steps aside. CONNER *picks up the scythe and starts to move to the door.*

PAIGE: Wait. Can I say good-bye to her?

CONNER: Ah . . . I don't think there's time . . .

She throws her arms around him.

PAIGE: I fucking love you guys.

CONNER: Yeah . . . me too.

He breaks the hug. A moment between them.

Um . . . so . . .

He suddenly kisses her. They kiss a moment, and slowly break apart.

PAIGE: Wow . . .

CONNER: I always wanted to do that!

PAIGE: You too?

CONNER: God . . . I was driving so fast cause I was gonna . . . you know, like, at the party . . .

PAIGE: Oh my God, this sucks! For like a million and one reasons.

His phone beeps again.

CONNER: Shit, I need to . . .

PAIGE: Go. Go get her. Um . . .

CONNER: So . . .

PAIGE: This really is . . .

CONNER: Don't say it. This is . . . I'll see you someday. On the other side.

They embrace once more and he finally breaks it. When he does, she watches him start to move to the door. Then, feeling something, places her hand on her chest, looks up and out to the audience, seeing something we don't. As CONNER places his hand on the doorknob, she inhales audibly. A big gasp, as if all of her breath were returning to her. Then, an intense flash of light. Then darkness. Then, dim lights. The two of them are gone, and the only thing that remains onstage is an open door.

END OF PLAY

PLAY SHAKESPEARE

George Freek

CHARACTERS
HANNAH: *17, playing Juliet.*
BRAD: *17, playing Romeo.*
BRUCE: *17, HANNAH's boyfriend.*
LUCY: *17, BRAD's girlfriend.*

TIME
The present.

SETTING
A bare rehearsal stage.

> *A bare rehearsal stage.* HANNAH *is temporarily alone; then* BRAD *enters.*

BRAD: Hi. What did you want to see me about?

HANNAH: Brad, I really think we need to rehearse some more.

BRAD: You do? You mean like right now?

HANNAH: Don't you have time?

BRAD: Well yeah, I guess so. But . . .

HANNAH: Good. Because I'm just not happy about the way it's going. I mean we don't seem to be connecting.

BRAD: Was this Mr. Jordan's suggestion?

HANNAH: No, it's my own idea. *Coy.* Do you like it?

BRAD: I just thought we were doing okay, and we do have two more weeks of rehearsal, you know.

HANNAH: I know, but I don't think we're really getting inside these characters. You know what I mean?

BRAD: I'm not sure.

HANNAH: Well look, they're two young kids, just like us, who are deeply in love with each other. Don't you think you could get a little more into that?

BRAD: So you think I'm not getting into my part? Is that what you're saying?

HANNAH: No, I just think you're holding back a little bit. *Coy.* Couldn't you just try a little harder?

BRAD: *Sighs.* I'll try.

HANNAH: *Sarcastic.* Thanks a lot.

BRAD: *Misses or skips the sarcasm.* Well, okay, where do you want to take it from?

HANNAH: How about if we start from act 2, scene 2, line 6, okay?

There is a long pause, during which BRAD *looks confused.*

You want me to cue you?

BRAD: No. I'm okay. I've got it. *Another pause.* Cue me.

HANNAH: *Psyching herself.*

"Therefore pardon me,

And not impute this yielding to light love,

Which the dark night hath so discovered."

BRAD: *Thinks.* Okay, I got it!

"Lady, by yonder blessed moon I vow,

That tips with silver all these fruit tree tops—"

HANNAH: "Oh swear not by the moon, th'inconstant moon,

That monthly changes in her circled orb,

Lest that thy love prove likewise variable."

BRAD: "What shall I swear by?"

HANNAH: "Do not swear at all;

Or if thou wilt, swear by thy gracious self,

Which is the god of my idolatry,

And I'll believe thee."

BRAD: "If my heart's dear love"—

HANNAH: Cut! Hold it, Brad. Now I don't mean to criticize . . .

BRAD: But you're going to, anyway.

HANNAH: No, but I mean if I am your "heart's dear love," could you think of me like that a little more. Is it that hard to do?

BRAD: *He "psychs" himself.* "If my heart's dear love"—

HANNAH: *Really getting into it.* "Well, do not swear. Although I joy in thee,

I have no joy in this contract tonight:

It is too rash, too unadvised, too sudden. Sweet, goodnight;

This bud of love, by summer's ripening breath,

May prove a beauteous flower when next we meet.

Goodnight, goodnight! As sweet repose and rest

Come to thy heart as that within my breast."

BRAD: *A little warmer.* "O wilt thou leave me so unsatisfied?"

HANNAH: *A little too suggestive.* "What satisfaction canst thou have tonight?"

BRAD: "Th'exchange of thy love's faithful vow for mine."

BRUCE *appears, unnoticed by* HANNAH *and* BRAD.

HANNAH: Look, why don't we improvise here?

BRAD: What do you mean?

HANNAH: Well look, wouldn't you like to kiss me?

BRAD: Wouldn't that be going too far?

HANNAH: *Coy.* I think we might even go a little further.

Pause.

BRAD: I don't think Mr. Jordan would agree.

HANNAH: We could just try it between ourselves.

BRAD: I think we better stick to the script.

HANNAH: *She smiles.* Just think about it.

Then, as Juliet:

"I gave thee mine before thou didst request it:

And yet, I wish it were to give again."

BRAD: "Wouldst thou then withdraw it? For what purpose, love?"

HANNAH: "Only to be frank and give it thee again:

And yet I wish but for the thing I have.

My bounty is as boundless as the sea,

My love is deep. The more I give to thee,

The more I have. For both are infinite.

But I hear some noise within. Dear love, adieu"—

She is about to kiss him now.

BRAD: I think the Nurse calls now, doesn't she?

And as if on cue, BRUCE *then steps in, slightly confused and annoyed.*

BRUCE: Hi.

HANNAH: *Annoyed.* Well, well! Here's our Nurse!

BRAD: Hi, Bruce.

BRUCE: Um, what's going on?

HANNAH: *Peeved.* What does it look like?

BRUCE: I don't know. That's why I thought I'd ask.

HANNAH: Brad and I are rehearsing the play, if you couldn't tell.

BRUCE: Oh yeah? *Sarcastically.* And what's the play, *Romeo and Juliet*?

HANNAH: That's right. It is.

BRUCE: Oh.

HANNAH: And you're interrupting us.

BRAD: But that's okay, Bruce. We're about finished, I think.

HANNAH: No we're not! We have a lot more work to do.

BRUCE: I'm sorry, but—look, I thought you wanted a ride to the mall, Hannah.

HANNAH: I changed my mind. This is more important.

BRUCE: That's okay. I have time to wait.

HANNAH: Don't bother. If I still want to go when we're finished, I can always get another ride—somewhere.

She looks expectantly at BRAD.

BRAD: Look, Hannah, if you really need to go to the mall, we can . . .

HANNAH: Don't be silly. This is way more important than anything I was going to do at the mall.

BRUCE: *Now vainly trying to assert himself.* Now just a minute, Hannah—I've been waiting around for you for like a half an hour. You never said anything to me about rehearsing this stupid play!

HANNAH: STUPID PLAY! I guess that shows what you know about Shakespeare!

BRUCE: *Looking at* BRAD. Well, I know about things that are right in front of my nose!

BRAD: *Quickly steps behind* BRUCE. He's got a point, Hannah.

HANNAH: He sure does. It's sitting right there on top of his head!

BRUCE: If that's the way you're going to be, I don't care if you have to walk to the mall!

HANNAH: If you'll be there, I don't want to go at all!

BRUCE: *To* BRAD. Well, I guess I can take a hint.

HANNAH: You call that a hint?

BRAD: Um, look, I think we should all . . .

BRUCE: Oh, forget it! I'm out of here!

He storms out. Pause.

BRAD: I'm sorry. That was unfortunate.

HANNAH: No, it's him! He is sooo dumb!

BRAD: But I thought you two were, you know, sort of going together.

HANNAH: Are you kidding? Football players! What can you do with them?

BRAD: I don't know. I never dated one.

She thinks this is hilarious.

HANNAH: Oh wow! You are sooo funny!

BRAD: I meant it.

HANNAH: The thing is, see, I didn't want to like hurt his feelings.

BRAD: You didn't?

HANNAH: Of course not, Brad—I mean I don't want to be cruel! But you tell me. What's a girl to do? He just keeps hanging around, and I'm really getting tired of it. He won't leave me alone, for heaven's sake! You'd think he'd have some pride, wouldn't you? Or have some respect for me, at least! He doesn't think about the position he's putting me in! He should realize how I feel. The truth is I feel really awful!

Suddenly she appears to be on the verge of tears. Pause.

BRAD: I don't know what to say.

And then suddenly LUCY *enters, smiling breezily.*

LUCY: Hi. What's this? More rehearsing, Hannah?

HANNAH: *Icily.* Hello, Lucy.

LUCY: So, how's it going?

HANNAH: We still have a lot of work to do.

LUCY: Oh. Well, if you're hard at it, I'll leave you to it. I'll see you later.

She starts to exit.

BRAD: Lucy, wait! I've had enough for one day. I'd like some refreshment. How about a Coke?

LUCY: Sure. Hannah?

BRAD: Hannah has a date to go to the mall. Let's go. I'm really thirsty.

They exit.

HANNAH: *Rather stunned.* Huh? *Pause.* Bruce, wait! I didn't mean it, Bruce!

She dashes off.

END OF PLAY

RED SUGARY
SWEET DREAMS

Daniel John Kelley

Kate Bell commissioned *Red Sugary Sweet Dreams* for The Lower Manhattan Arts Academy (LoMA) in October of 2013. It was produced and performed at LoMA in December of 2013 as part of Selfies. It was directed by Heather Cambanes and performed by the following cast:

AMBER: Clarice Lennon
JESSICA: Kristen Feliciano
RODERICK, THE KOOL-AID MAN: Julian Baez

CHARACTERS

AMBER: *In her teens, a guarded dreamer.*

JESSICA: *In her teens, an effusive dreamer.*

RODERICK, THE KOOL-AID MAN: *In his teens, the dashing, heroic Kool-Aid man of everyone's dreams.*

TIME

The present. At the end of the day, at sunset.

SETTING

Outside a high school, and in the mind of dreamers.

> JESSICA *and* AMBER *are standing together.* AMBER *is texting, waiting for a response, looking morose.* JESSICA *is texting. She gets a response. She smiles, broadly. She turns to* AMBER.

JESSICA: So. I have a secret dream.

AMBER: A what?

JESSICA: A dream I've never told anybody in the whole of my life and that means the world to me.

> *Beat.*

AMBER: So . . . what? You're going to tell me it now and . . .

JESSICA: Yes. Because you're my best friend.

AMBER: Okay. Stop. That's a lot of pressure.

JESSICA: No, it's not.

AMBER: No, no, it is. I don't want to be the only holder of your "secret dream."

JESSICA: Why not?

AMBER: Because what if I think it's stupid.

JESSICA: You won't.

AMBER: I might! You don't know. I don't know! You've never told anybody. You're just holding this precious thing in, and, like, that's okay, but if you share it out to the world, then it becomes subject to like, the judgment of the world. And the people in the world. And that is something that most of the time usually sucks.

JESSICA: You had a secret dream.

AMBER: What?

JESSICA: Amber. Don't lie. You had a secret dream. Or maybe you still have it?

AMBER *looks at* JESSICA. AMBER *turns to go.*

AMBER: Yeah . . . I gotta go.

JESSICA: Oh crap, you do, you do, you do, and you told someone, and they thought it was stupid. Am I wrong?

AMBER: My mom, she, you know, she gets crazy if I'm late, and . . .

JESSICA: You don't have to shut me out, Amber.

AMBER: I'm not, I'm actually concerned about my mother, is that so insane . . .

JESSICA *moves in front of* AMBER. *She places her hands on* AM-BER's *shoulders.*

JESSICA: You can tell me this thing. You can tell it to me and I will celebrate your dream with you.

AMBER: You won't.

JESSICA: Look at me. How long have we known each other?

AMBER: Not that long. Like a year and a half.

JESSICA: Okay. But, like, we understand each other.

AMBER: I guess.

JESSICA: When you were on your special lady time and you were going out with your family later and you needed other pants, did I or did I not give you the pants off my legs?

AMBER: We were at your house.

JESSICA: Did I or did I not do that?

AMBER: Yes! You did! You gave me your pants! And you didn't even give me a funny look when I didn't give them back for like four months! But you don't even know what you're asking here . . .

JESSICA: It doesn't matter. You tell me your secret dream and I'll tell you mine and we'll be really amazingly excited for each other. I swear this, on my little brother's life.

AMBER: . . . Whoa.

JESSICA: Yeah. I'm serious.

A moment. AMBER *moves from* JESSICA. *She takes a breath. She turns to* JESSICA.

AMBER: It's just . . . I told my boyfriend once and he laughed at me. Like for five minutes straight. We were in the park, and he almost fell off the bench. People were looking at us. He just sat there and laughed at me, like, "That's what you've been holding in all this time. Just that."

JESSICA: He's dumb.

AMBER: He is. I like him, but . . .

JESSICA: It's not a forever thing.

AMBER: Definitely not.

She takes a deep breath. She psyches herself up. She looks to the sky.

Okay . . . I grew up here in the city. Like you. But . . . I haven't really ever been anywhere else. I mean, sometimes I go to Brooklyn or Queens, to like see friends or whatever, but . . . there's a part of me that really wants to like . . . see the world.

JESSICA: That's great!

AMBER: I'm not finished!

JESSICA: Okay!

AMBER: This is really, really hard!

JESSICA: Okay, I'll, shut up, okay . . .

AMBER: Okay. So. A lot of people picked on me when I was younger. And still pick on me, because I'm shy and a little weird sometimes. And, like . . . the happiest memories I have of elementary school, are the quiet ones, when everyone else was off running around, playing or laughing or doing something dumb, and they left me all alone. I got to sit there, in the quiet, on the concrete, and eat my lunch . . . and drink my Kool-Aid drink. I didn't have a lot of friends in elementary school. Or middle school. Or like, even now, I don't have that many friends.

JESSICA: Come on.

AMBER: I don't, not real ones. Not ones I actually like on a regular basis like you.

JESSICA: Wow. Thank you.

AMBER: Yeah. Okay. So. In elementary school, as I sat on the concrete, and as I drank my Kool-Aid drink, I looked at the, uh . . .

She takes a deep breath. She closes her eyes.

I looked at the red Kool-Aid guy on the juice box and I imagined he was my friend when no one else was. . . . And sometimes . . . I imagined he was even more than that.

JESSICA covers her mouth, amazed. A moment. AMBER looks away, smiling at last, getting lost in her reverie . . . A vision of the KOOL-AID MAN appears, smiling at AMBER.

KOOL-AID MAN: OHHHH YEAH!

AMBER: I imagined that the red Kool-Aid guy would pick me up after school and take me away . . . from everything!

The KOOL-AID MAN approaches, and takes AMBER by the hand. They run away! As she describes the scene, they enact it.

We would go, far from the school yard, and Manhattan and even New York State, and we would travel south, far south, to Hastings, South Carolina, where Kool-Aid was invented, and there I'd start again. He'd take me to his Kool-Aid school, and I'd meet all his Kool-Aid friends, and they'd all like me and wouldn't make fun of me or think I was weird, and we'd all just know each other so, so well, all of us, and we'd understand what we were all going through all the time, because of Kool-Aid, and I'd be so incredibly happy every day! And then, when night came, we new friends would all go our separate ways, and the two us, the Kool-Aid guy and me, we would go out walking in the North Carolina woods, where the sky is full of stars, and underneath an old oak tree, he'd pull me close and, whisper in my ear, saying . . .

AMBER and KOOL-AID MAN: "Amber . . . is it all right if I kiss you now?"

AMBER: And we'd kiss, so quietly and so tenderly . . . and then go off, into the bushes and . . .

She closes her eyes and imagines. The KOOL-AID MAN smiles at her.

KOOL-AID MAN: Oh yeeeeah . . .

The KOOL-AID MAN is gone. A moment. AMBER looks down at the ground. She doesn't look at JESSICA.

AMBER: That last part is kind of a recent addition to the whole thing, actually, so . . .

She turns on JESSICA, *laughing at herself, bitterly.*

HA HA HA! PRETTY DUMB, RIGHT?

JESSICA *reaches out a hand to her.*

JESSICA: No. No. It isn't. Oh my God . . .

AMBER: What?

JESSICA: I think that's so beautiful . . .

AMBER: Shut up. You don't.

JESSICA: No, I do. I do!

AMBER: You can't! You're just screwing around and . . .

JESSICA: I'm not! I swear!

AMBER: STOP IT!

JESSICA: I can't believe this. But . . . all you just said . . . That's my secret dream too, Amber! Almost exactly!

AMBER: Really?

JESSICA: Yes! YES, OH MY GOD! I sat alone on the concrete, and I drank Kool-Aid, and I dreamt the exact same thing, every day! It's just, it's like you're in MY MIND and in MY LIFE! It's so WEIRD!

AMBER: It's not. It's not weird. We both feel it.

JESSICA: We both do.

AMBER: You swear? You're not . . .

JESSICA: On my little brother's life. Again.

They look at each other. They embrace.

AMBER: This is the best day ever . . .

JESSICA: For me too . . .

They hold each other. JESSICA *pulls away.*

It's just . . . I . . .

AMBER: What?

JESSICA: I don't know how to say this, but . . .

AMBER: Just say it. Anything. Nothing can change what just happened, here, on the street, outside our school, between two friends, NOTHING . . .

Suddenly, the KOOL-AID MAN *enters, swiftly. He moves to* JESSICA.

KOOL-AID MAN: My love! The ship awaits! We sail at sunset for Hastings, South Carolina! There we will begin again at my Kool-Aid school, with my Kool-Aid friends. And one night, while walking alone in the North Carolina woods, the sky full of stars, I will pull you close underneath an old oak tree and . . .

He notices AMBER. *He turns to her, and bows, politely.*

Oh, I'm sorry. I don't think we've met. My name is Roderick, the Kool-Aid man.

He extends his hand.

AMBER: Roderick?

KOOL-AID MAN: Yes. As was my father before me.

AMBER *turns.*

AMBER: Roderick. I never knew his name . . .

JESSICA: In my dream, he was always Roderick . . .

JESSICA *and* RODERICK *look at each other.* AMBER *falls to a knee.*

I am so, so sorry, Amber. I had no idea. Seriously. This all happened so fast, I had been dreaming of it for years, and then we met last week, and it was him, and I was like "YOU!" and he was like "YOU!" and it was like electric, and I was going to tell you tonight—that was what my secret was all about—and then you said, well, I didn't know you had all that inside you, and I had no idea it was going to be exactly the . . .

AMBER: It might have been better if you laughed at me.

JESSICA: Amber.

AMBER: Give me a minute . . .

KOOL-AID MAN: My love, is there something terribly the matter?

AMBER: "My love . . . "!

KOOL-AID MAN: Your friend, she . . .

JESSICA: Maybe you better go . . . for now . . .

KOOL-AID MAN: The tide awaits . . .

JESSICA: I know . . .

KOOL-AID MAN: If we don't go now we will lose the wind, and by the time we can take ship again your parents will have discovered you're gone and all will be . . .

AMBER *turns back, with great force, smiling through tears.*

AMBER: No, no, there's no problem here, Roderick. No, not at all! You must go. Both of you . . .

JESSICA: Amber . . .

AMBER: The only thing the matter here is that some people in this world have dreams that stay dreams and some see those dreams burst into bloom, but who are we stay-dreamers to wish ill fortune on our friends in fullest bloom? Why should there not be a little happiness in this world for some, if not for others?

JESSICA: I don't have to go away.

KOOL-AID MAN: My love . . .

JESSICA: Roderick, please . . .

AMBER: No . . .

AMBER *takes* JESSICA *by the hand.*

For years, I have lived and felt so alone in all I thought and dreamed. But today, I felt—for one brief fleeting glimmering moment—that someone understood me. And that someone was you, Jessica. For a minute, both our blood was full of red sugary sweet dreams. And even if you go now, that moment will still live in my heart. Today, I am a little less alone. And here I see yet still further proof of that moment's realness—my best friend and my imagined love, now real, are to set off and make a reality of that which, until this afternoon, seemed only the stupid imaginings of my deep loneliness. Jessica. My best friend. Go now to Hastings, South Carolina. Go, drink Kool-Aid, and be happy.

JESSICA: Will you be all right, Amber?

AMBER: I will try to be. I will dump my crappy boyfriend tomorrow, and I will try.

AMBER *and* JESSICA *embrace one last time.*

JESSICA: Thank you. Thank you, Amber. I'll miss you.

AMBER: I'll miss you too.

KOOL-AID MAN: And I . . . I will be sad not to know you better,

Amber, best friend of my love. If only . . .

AMBER: It was never to be, Roderick. Never. Not even as friends. I wish you both only the best . . .

> JESSICA *and the* KOOL-AID MAN *hold hands, and go, waving to* AMBER.

JESSICA: Good-bye!

KOOL-AID MAN: Good-bye!

AMBER: Good-bye!

JESSICA: *Offstage.* Good-bye!

AMBER: Good-bye . . .

JESSICA: *Offstage.* Bye, Amber! I'll never forget you!

> AMBER *watches them go, smiling and waving. As they go,* AMBER's *smile fades. They're gone. A moment.* AMBER *reaches behind her, and, slowly, carefully pulls out a box of Kool-Aid. She looks at it, longingly. She takes the straw out of the packaging. She punctures the juice box. She drinks long, closing her eyes, dreaming, smiling . . . After a moment, she tosses it aside, takes out her phone, and exits, texting. She smiles, softly, sadly, to herself. Blackout.*

END OF PLAY

THE RISING COST OF VINYL
Mark Rigney

CHARACTERS

CRYSTAL: *a high school sophomore. She is* AUSTIN*'s sister; she knows her brother very well.*

AUSTIN: *a high school senior. He is* CRYSTAL*'s brother; he intends to impress.*

MARIA: *a high school sophomore. She is* CRYSTAL*'s friend; she is perceptive.*

TIME

Yesterday, after school.

SETTING

A basement. Several boxes or storage trunks. A work light, maybe attached to a sawhorse. Also, a number of vinyl records, at least some of them in protective plastic sleeves, and at least a couple that are mimicking rare and collectible editions.

> AUSTIN*'s and* CRYSTAL*'s basement. Except it's really their parents' basement. A group of boxes or storage chests dominates the space. Approaching the mess are three teens—*AUSTIN, CRYSTAL *and* MARIA*—bearing flashlights.* AUSTIN *carries a backpack containing a laptop and a book: a dog-eared collector's guide to pricing vinyl records.*

AUSTIN: *Aiming his flashlight at one particular box.* There. That one.

CRYSTAL: So you're like burglarizing our own house.

AUSTIN: Crystal, chill. I just like to know what's what.

CRYSTAL: If you've been getting into my stuff? I swear I will text, tweet, and Facebook you to death.

AUSTIN: I don't go into your room and you know it.

CRYSTAL: I will bury you in rumors five miles deep.

AUSTIN: I heard you the first time.

MARIA: Hey, I'm feeling a little creeped out, so I'm just going to . . .

AUSTIN: Whoa, wait, Maria. Don't go. This is worth seeing.

MARIA: *To Crystal.* You said we were going to Dairy Queen.

CRYSTAL: And we will. But until the rain lets up, and since Austin's so gung-ho to show us this whatever it is . . .

MARIA: I don't like the dark.

AUSTIN: I don't think the overhead's working, but this won't take long, okay?

MARIA: It doesn't bother you? Darkness?

AUSTIN: Sure—but then I realized that when I was in the dark, I was part of the dark, and I'm not afraid of myself, so that kind of ended that.

MARIA: Wow. That must be incredible.

AUSTIN: What?

MARIA: Not being afraid of yourself.

AUSTIN: Okay, look, we can at least get a work light or something, here.

He gets the work light on. Not bright, but better than nothing.

There. See? Nothing to worry about.

CRYSTAL: My, aren't we gallant today.

AUSTIN: Just look in the box.

CRYSTAL *hauls out an old vinyl record album.*

CRYSTAL: So this is what you're just dying to show us?

AUSTIN: That's it.

CRYSTAL: Why?

AUSTIN: Because they're worth some serious money.

CRYSTAL: This? Get out.

AUSTIN: Maybe not that one, no. But some . . .

CRYSTAL: Even if they are. They're not ours.

AUSTIN: Possession is nine-tenths of the law.

CRYSTAL: And just who are you quoting that from?

MARIA: I like the artwork. I mean, that's wild.

CRYSTAL: I've seen worse, I guess.

MARIA: So these are all, like, your dad's?

AUSTIN: Not any more.

MARIA: My uncle collects records. Not this kind, though.

AUSTIN: What kind?

MARIA: Tex-Mex, Tejano. If you've got any of that, old forty-fives, he'd be wanting to hear from you.

CRYSTAL: Oh, listen to you. Talkin' the talk, "Old forty-fives" and stuff.

MARIA: Y'know, I can go to Dairy Queen on my own.

CRYSTAL: *Teasing.* Not if it's dark.

MARIA: *Not unkindly.* Which it isn't, so shut up.

AUSTIN: *To Maria.* Hey, you like the old covers? Look at this one, check that out.

CRYSTAL: Austin, give me a break. You don't care about artwork.

AUSTIN: Says who? I mean, look at this thing.

CRYSTAL: Austin.

AUSTIN: Okay, yes, there is a larger purpose.

CRYSTAL: Which is?

AUSTIN: I knew Dad had been pretty serious once upon a time, so when I found these, I wrote some things down, right? And then I checked online, and I was just about jumping out of my chair.

CRYSTAL: You already said that.

AUSTIN: No. I mean really valuable.

CRYSTAL: Really valuable meaning what?

AUSTIN: Thousands. Like many, many thousands.

CRYSTAL: For true?

> AUSTIN *hauls out a record in a protective plastic sleeve. He angles it so* MARIA *has the best view.*

AUSTIN: Look, look at this one. The Beatles. Common as dirt, right? But not with this cover. This is the butcher cover, see? The dead baby dolls, the blood? And it's mint, inside and out. Still in the shrink-wrap.

CRYSTAL: Can I see, too, please?

MARIA: And this is worth . . . what?

AUSTIN: According to this price guide, eight to twelve thousand.

CRYSTAL: Excuse me?

AUSTIN: It came out in 1966, it was only on the shelves for a couple of days, and people got so angry, the record company pulled it and pasted new covers on. So an original, without the paste-on—I mean, we're talking about the Beatles, the Beatles where they made a mistake, and when people like that blow it in public, that means big money.

MARIA: I like it. The way they're smiling, even with all that blood. It's all—you know—what is it? Irony.

CRYSTAL: It's gross.

AUSTIN: You don't have to like it. The point is, it's valuable, and there's more. Weird mono editions, Japanese pressings, bands no one's ever heard of . . .

CRYSTAL: Does Mom know this is down here?

AUSTIN: I think she's too upset to remember.

MARIA: So your dad skips out, and you're gonna sell his stuff to get back at him?

AUSTIN: And to make some money, yeah.

MARIA: If I had this, I wouldn't sell. I'd hang it on my bedroom wall.

AUSTIN: You'd hang twelve grand on your wall? To look at?

MARIA: It's a piece of history.

AUSTIN: A very valuable piece, yes! And way too ugly for your bedroom wall.

MARIA: Oh, I don't know. I'd probably have to take down the Giger or the Eulsmann to make room, or maybe the Warhol . . .

AUSTIN: You have an original Warhol?

MARIA: No. Just a poster. You know, the banana.

CRYSTAL: See, Austin, I know you don't get this, but Maria is not a girl who does teddy bears and hearts.

AUSTIN: Either way. None of us can afford this on our wall.

MARIA: So you'd rather have the cash, that's cool. But what would you spend it on?

AUSTIN: I don't know. We could get a car with this. A new stereo. More iPhones than even my sister'd know what to do with.

CRYSTAL: What kind of car?

AUSTIN: How 'bout a rag-top? How 'bout a vintage T-bird convertible?

CRYSTAL: Huh.

AUSTIN: Huh? What huh?

CRYSTAL: You'd look pretty sharp, showing up to prom in a T-bird.

AUSTIN: Yes. Yes, I would.

CRYSTAL: And even sharper with Maria here in a really gorgeous dress, decorating the front seat.

AUSTIN, *glowering at* CRYSTAL, *fails to respond.*

MARIA: Oh, I get it!

CRYSTAL: Yeah, so do I.

MARIA: No, it's kind of sweet.

To AUSTIN*:*

If I'd known you got me down here to impress me, I could have made it easier on you.

AUSTIN: Oh, really.

MARIA: I could have at least pretended we were on the same wavelength.

CRYSTAL: C'mon, girlfriend. I hear a DQ Blizzard calling our name.

MARIA: Look, Austin, if I had this box in my basement? No matter who screwed me over, I wouldn't be just selling it off. I mean, you're right, I've met your dad, he's a jerk. But that doesn't mean you have to act like him.

AUSTIN: Excuse me?

MARIA: It's theft. Taking something that isn't yours and selling it, that's theft.

AUSTIN: Maria! I'm in my own house!

MARIA: What are they always saying on that one show? "It's black-letter law."

AUSTIN: Okay, seriously. You can go now. Both of you.

CRYSTAL: Wait a minute. What if we sell these, yeah, but what if we don't keep the money?

AUSTIN: What are you talking about?

CRYSTAL: What if we give it away, to something good, like that playground fund, or the Red Cross?

AUSTIN: Give it away? Crystal, this is free money!

CRYSTAL: Yeah, it is. So what have we got to lose?

MARIA: And it still sends a big "up yours" to your runaway dad, if that's what you're after. But this way, you stay on the straight and narrow.

AUSTIN: Oh, listen to the future PhD in ethics.

MARIA: I'm starting to think you would not make a very good prom date.

CRYSTAL: Hang on. Austin. I'm serious.

AUSTIN: Do you have any conception of how much money is wrapped up in this one box? And there are three more like it, at least!

CRYSTAL: Hey, so we could have the whole school over for a party, hire a bartender, the works. Or we could do what dad never would have done, ever, and do something nice for, I don't know . . .

MARIA: . . . for charity . . .

CRYSTAL: Exactly, that's right, for charity. For people in need.

AUSTIN: Why can't we do something nice for us?

CRYSTAL: You know what? I bet that when the Beatles made this cover, they thought it was a good idea. Funny or whatever. But then it turned out it was a bad idea, and they had to suck it up and deal. So I'm looking at you, big brother. I'm looking at you with a potentially really great idea and a major opportunity to blow it. And I admit, I would like a new car. That box could maybe take me straight from my learner's permit to a Jaguar. But I gotta ask, is that the kind of car I want to drive?

AUSTIN: What are you talking about? Jaguar's a decent car.

MARIA: But not for thirty pieces of silver.

AUSTIN: Thirty pieces . . . ? I just asked you to prom, and you're calling me Judas?

MARIA: Well, first off, you didn't actually ask me, and second . . .

CRYSTAL: Maria. Just leave it alone.

MARIA: You're right. And I am starting to hear that Blizzard calling . . .

CRYSTAL: Smooth like Maxwell.

MARIA: Bruno Mars.

AUSTIN: You are both certifiable.

CRYSTAL: No, don't stop, don't engage, keep walking.

MARIA: 'Bye, Austin. Thanks for showing me the basement.

Both girls exit. A moment. Then AUSTIN *opens his laptop.*

AUSTIN: Fine. Open eBay. Sell. Your. Item. Enter.

As the lights come down, we hear (ideally) the opening of the Beatles' "Nowhere Man."

END OF PLAY

RMEO + JULEZ

Michael Salomon

Rmeo + Julez was the winner of 2009 MTC/Dentyne National Student Play-writing Competition. It was produced by Manhattan Theatre Club on May 14, 2009. The director was Andy Goldberg. The cast was as follows:

ROMEO: Utkarsh Ambudkar
JULIET: Shirley A. Rumierk

CHARACTERS

JULIET: *The classic Juliet—a teenager, dressed in her nightgown, lovely as the sunset (or Taylor Swift).*

ROMEO: *The classic Romeo—a teenager, more lover than fighter (probably listens to indie), dressed in the clothes that he wore to the night's masquerade.*

TIME

A warm summer evening.

SETTING

JULIET*'s balcony and courtyard in Verona, Italy.*

A warm summer evening. JULIET *stands at the edge of her balcony.* ROMEO *lingers in the grassy courtyard below.*

JULIET: Oh Romeo, Romeo.

Wherefore art thou, Romeo?

Deny thy father and refuse thy name,

Or if thou wilt not, be but sworn my love,

And I'll no longer be a Capulet.

ROMEO: I take thee at thy word.

Call me but love and I'll be new baptized.

Henceforth I never will be Romeo.

JULIET: What man art thou that, thus bescreened in night,

So stumblest on my counsel?

ROMEO: By a name

I know not how to tell thee who I am.

My name, dear saint, is . . .

    Her cell phone begins to ring. Pause.

My name, dear saint, is . . .

    The cell phone is still ringing.

JULIET: I should probably get that.

ROMEO: Of course.

    JULIET *pulls out a cell phone. Into phone:*

JULIET: Hello? . . . Oh, hi Tybalt. . . . Yeah, I'm good. I did. I had a great time. Look . . . No I didn't know, but listen, I . . . your sword? . . . Well I'm sure that'll teach him to bite his thumb at you then.

She mouths, "I'm sorry" to ROMEO. *Back to phone:*

Look—look, Tybalt, now really isn't a good time. . . . No, I'm at home. It's just that . . . I know. I know. We'll do something soon—I promise. It's just been such a crazy week for me with the masquerade and you know. . . yes, you're absolutely right. . . . Fine, brunch on Tuesday sounds great. I really got to go. . . . No, nurse is calling me right now. . . . She is not! Don't say things like that about her. . . . Fine. I have to go, we'll discuss later. . . . Okay. . . . Bye.

She hangs up the phone.

Sorry. My cousin.

ROMEO: No worries.

JULIET: Shall we?

ROMEO: Of course.

Clears his throat.

I know not how to tell thee who I am.

My name, dear saint, is hateful to myself

Because it is an enemy to thee.

Had I it written, I . . .

JULIET's phone rings again.

JULIET: Oh my God, I'm so sorry.

ROMEO: It's fine.

JULIET: Seriously, no one ever calls me. This is like some freak occurrence.

ROMEO: Uh huh.

JULIET checks her phone.

JULIET: It's my mom.

ROMEO: Go ahead.

JULIET picks up the phone.

JULIET: Hey Mom. . . . No, I'm in the house. What do you need? . . . Yeah, I had a great time . . . Yes, I saw him. Very charming . . .

What? . . . What? . . . Where did you hear that? . . . I was not . . .

She casts a glance at ROMEO *and whispers into the phone:*

I was not kissing any. . . I don't know where you heard something like that, but whoever . . .

Normal volume:

Mom . . . Mom, that's ridiculous . . . That's none of your business . . . Because I'm fourteen, that's why. I'm allowed to make those decisions myself, okay? Look, can we please not talk about this right now? . . . Mom, we'll talk about it later. I need to . . . Nobody's here . . . Who would be here right now? . . . Yes, that's right, Mom, I'm inviting strange men into our house . . . No. Goodnight, Mom . . . Goodnight, Mom . . . Goodnight . . . Love you too.

She hangs up the phone.

Oh my God.

ROMEO: Moms?

JULIET: Tell me about it.

ROMEO: Everything okay?

JULIET: Oh yeah. She's just . . . you know.

ROMEO: Uh huh.

JULIET: Um, you were saying something about your name being an enemy to me.

ROMEO: Right. Um. . . My name. . . it is an enemy to thee.

Had I it written, I would tear the word.

JULIET: My ears have yet not drunk a hundred words

Of thy tongue's uttering, yet I know the sound.

Art thou not Ro—. . .

Her phone rings again. A different tone.

ROMEO: Oh for God's sake.

JULIET: I'm sorry. Really.

ROMEO: It's okay. Just answer it.

She takes out the phone.

JULIET: It's just a text.

ROMEO: Ah.

She looks at the text. Makes a face.

JULIET: Oh God.

ROMEO: What?

JULIET: It's just from this guy. Ech.

ROMEO: This guy?

JULIET: Yeah, this guy, Paris. God, he will not leave me alone. It's like every night with him—like clockwork or something.

She starts to reply to the text.

And of course my parents adore him, so you know how that is.

ROMEO: Totally. So is there, like, anything, um, going on between you guys, then?

JULIET: Going on between . . .? Ooooh! No, no, no. Not right now. Just . . . friends. Hardly even.

ROMEO: Not right now?

JULIET: Well, like I said, my folks are really pushing for this to happen, but I am not into him at all. So no: nothing going on there.

ROMEO: Cool.

JULIET: Yeah.

She finishes the text and puts the phone away.

Sorry about that.

ROMEO: Not to worry.

JULIET: Right. Um. . . . How cam'st thou hither, tell me, and wherefore?

The orchard walls are high and hard to climb,

And the place death, considering who thou art,

If any of my kinsmen . . .

ROMEO*'s phone begins to ring. He sighs in frustration.* JULIET *takes her phone out and checks it.*

That's not me.

ROMEO: Oh crud.

He takes out his phone and looks at it.

I don't know the number.

JULIET: Could be important.

ROMEO: Do you mind?

JULIET: How could I?

ROMEO: Right. Thanks.

He answers the phone.

Hello? . . . Hi, who is this? . . . Oh! Rosaline! Yeah. . . . No, I, um, just got a new phone so I don't have all the numbers programmed . . . Well of course I wouldn't delete it. No, that's ridiculous . . . We are still friends . . . Look, I completely understand, but right now isn't a good time for . . . I—I don't know when it'll be a good time . . . Because I'm busy right now. Look, I really have to go . . . No, I'm not with anybody, I just can't talk . . . Because I can't, okay? . . . I'll call you . . . Yes, I have your number now . . . Yes, okay? . . . Okay. Bye.

He hangs up his phone.

JULIET: Rosaline?

ROMEO: Just an old friend.

JULIET: An old friend?

ROMEO: Yeah.

JULIET: Whose number you deleted? Ouch.

ROMEO: I didn't delete . . . Okay. Fine, she was kind of sort of an old flame. Things didn't really end well. I may have taken her out of my phonebook.

JULIET: I guess that's good news then.

ROMEO: Good news?

JULIET: For me.

ROMEO: Oh. Uh, right. Then . . . um . . . With love's light wings did I o'erperch these walls,

For stony limits cannot hold love out,

And what love can do, that dares love attempt.

Therefore . . .

JULIET's phone rings.

Man, you are just one popular girl tonight.

JULIET: Look, I'm sorry.

She checks her phone.

Oh shoot, I was supposed to call this guy back. Do you mind? This is the last one. I promise.

ROMEO: Go ahead.

JULIET *answers the phone.*

JULIET: Hey Sampson. How are you? . . . I know. I know. I'm so sorry I forgot. Things just got crazy, you know? . . . I know. You're right.

ROMEO*'s phone begins to ring.*

Yeah, no—I know. Gregory told me . . . Really?

ROMEO *answers his phone.* ROMEO *and* JULIET *are talking on the phone simultaneously.*

ROMEO: *Into phone.* Whatup, Mercutio. . . . nah, I'm still here. . . . Because you guys were being a bunch of dicks . . . Yeah, I'm in her courtyard . . . Oh grow up . . . No, I'm literally in her courtyard . . . Juliet . . . Ju-li-et . . . You remember her. The brunette with the really nice . . . yeah, that one . . . No, I'm just—we're standing here talking . . . Yeah, just talking . . . Maybe because I'm a gentleman . . . Well we're not all you, are we? . . . No . . . No, forget Rosaline. That's over . . . Yeah, yeah, I know . . . Fine. You were right, I was wrong. Are you happy now? . . . Of course not . . . She's totally different. . . . Well for starters she's the most . . . No I can . . . Hello? You're still. . . Okay. Okay . . . *Now* I can . . . All I'm saying is if you'd just think for like two seconds. She's the

JULIET: *Into phone.* Well it does sound like you guys sort of instigated the thing. . . . No, see, that's just silly. . . . Yeah, but that's not grounds for— . . . I don't care what family they're from. You can't just go around drawing your sword every time there's a— . . . no, I'm not taking their side. I'm just saying— . . . Because who the hell cares if he's a Montague? . . . Oh yeah, and my dad's just the picture of mental stability to emulate. . . . I said my dad's just the picture . . . Hello? . . . Hello? Yeah, you're breaking up. . . No I can—Hello? You're still— . . . Ok. Ok. . . . *Now* I can. . . . All I'm saying is if you'd just think for like, two seconds . . . then maybe you'd realize how idiodic you look most . . . beautiful girl I have ever laid eyes on. . . . Shut up . . . Shut up . . . You have no idea how . . . That's gross. Come on, man . . . Look, I kind of have to go . . . I'll be back soon . . . Yeah, I'll give you a play by play . . . No . . . Alright, man. See ya. swinging that blade around at the drop of a hat . . . Yeah, I'm sure you do. I . . . Hello? . . . Hello? . . . Look, I'm losing you again . . . I'm gonna go. We'll talk about this another time . . . Okay? . . . Okay? . . . Bye.

Both hang up their phones.

ROMEO: Well. . .

JULIET: Sorry about that.

ROMEO: No problem.

JULIET: That's it. I'm putting mine on Silent.

ROMEO: Actually, it's getting kind of late. . .

JULIET: Oh.

ROMEO: So I think I'm gonna head out.

JULIET: Yeah, I understand.

ROMEO: But this was fun.

JULIET: Oh yeah. Totally.

ROMEO: Look, I uh, I think you're pretty cute, and, I mean, really cool, so I was kind of wondering . . . do you think I could get your number?

JULIET: Yeah. Of course.

ROMEO *takes out his phone.*

It's 917-555-2813.

ROMEO: Cool.

JULIET: Actually, do you want to call mine, so I can . . .?

ROMEO: Oh yeah. Sure. Calling right now.

He presses Send. A pause. JULIET*'s phone rings. She looks down at it.*

JULIET: Got it.

They both put away their phones.

ROMEO: Awesome. So then I'll give you a call sometime.

JULIET: Sounds good to me.

ROMEO: Great. Well, goodnight.

JULIET: Goodnight.

ROMEO: Bye.

JULIET: Bye.

> ROMEO *begins to walk off.* JULIET *watches him for a moment before pulling out her phone and excitedly starting to text.*

ROMEO: *Suddenly, grandly.* Sleep dwell upon thine eyes . . .

> *He spins around to finish the line toward her, but sees that she is focused on her texting.*

> *Half-heartedly, to himself:*

. . . peace in thy breast.

> *He exits. Lights down.*

END OF PLAY

SECOND KISS

Andrea Lepcio

Second Kiss was originally produced by the Vital Theatre in 2005, and was directed by Stephanie Gilman, with Ellen Crowley-Etten, Jenny Gammello, Jenna Kalinowski, and Will Reynolds at the Samuel French Off-Off Broadway Short Play Festival.

CHARACTERS
ME: *a just-turned-16-year-old girl.*
BEST FRIEND: *an 8th-grade girl.*
BOY: *a 17-year-old boy.*
GIRL: *an 18-year-old girl.*

TIME
Any Time and Not So Distant Past.

SETTINGS
School Yard
Coffee Shop
Down the Path

NOTE: Since most one-act festivals involve many actors, many of whom are young, the play calls for as many couples as the company can spare to make out, hook up, and otherwise flirt around the main character.

   A school yard.

ME: I am sweet, sweet sixteen and I have never been, never been, never. A lot of things actually never mind kissed which I haven't cause I don't count "seven minutes in heaven" rubbing dry lips mush mush with Steven Kurtz in the fifth grade or my cousin Barry's bar mitzvah when the DJ made us play dance/freeze and his obnoxious girlfriend Karen got the bright idea to stick me and Mitchell Drecker's braces together. I've never been kissed. And, really, see, I don't . . . I don't even get it. Kissing. his . . . I don't know. This wanting to kiss . . . maybe I'm retarded.

   As many actors as the company can spare make out, hook up, and otherwise flirt.

   Back then, eighth grade.

BEST FRIEND: Lora Tosk went all the way.

ME: All the way where?

BEST FRIEND: She did it.

ME: Did what?

BEST FRIEND: With a sophomore.

ME: I don't understand, I don't understand.

BEST FRIEND: Lora Tosk had sex.

ME: You mean . . .

BEST FRIEND: Yeah.

ME: Like with a . . .

BEST FRIEND: Penis.

ME: I had to think about that a lot. A lot and still, to this day, when I see Lora Tosk . . . I mean, every single time, even now, years later when I don't see her every day but only just Tuesdays and Thursdays in Spanish. Every time I see her all I think is Lora Tosk *había sexo en octova grado.* I understood the principle. The procedure in theory, but I still didn't, don't have any feel for it or interest, which is very confusing to not at all give a shit about something that most every other person I know and like the rest of the planet . . .

The frolicking gets serious.

. . . it's not like I haven't tried. It's not like I haven't explored my hand brushing by my nipples under my sheet. I've reached all the way down to like find the parts. My parts. And the nipples or whatever I briefly brush. Probably too briefly. Feeling something disconnected from anything I know. But liking a little bit the idea of someone telling me to do something as in making me.

BOY *breaks out of another girl's arms, turns to* ME.

BOY: Come here. Watcha doing?

ME: Sitting. Nothing. Going.

BOY: So like that was weird with your party, your parents being there.

ME: They surprised me.

BOY: And then they stayed.

ME: It was my birthday.

BOY: Weird.

ME: I guess.

BOY: How'd they even get you to the party?

ME: Uh . . . they just took me to the restaurant.

BOY: But how'd they like know where you were?

ME: I was home.

BOY: Don't you go out?

ME: Sure, yeah, sometimes.

BOY: You want to go?

ME: Right now?

BOY: Yes.

ME: Where?

BOY: I don't know.

ME: Oh.

BOY: Get a soda.

ME: I guess.

ME *and* BOY *walk away from the "school yard" to a "coffee shop."*

BOY: A raspberry lime rickey. Why are you laughing?

ME: It's just a joke. My best friend. From my old school. We used to call it. Back in eighth grade. We used to go to Friendly's and we'd call it . . . I don't know, one of us made a mistake one time so we called it a raspberry lime lickey.

BOY: A lickey.

ME: Stupid.

BOY: I like lickeys.

ME: Yeah.

BOY: Do you like lickeys?

ME: I like ginger ale better.

BOY: Let's sit at the counter.

ME: I've never been here.

BOY: No?

ME: We don't come here. We haven't.

BOY: Who?

ME: My family. My parents, I guess.

BOY: Do you go everywhere with them?

ME: No. Sometimes. Well like . . .

BOY: One raspberry lime lickey, please.

ME: One raspberry lime rickey.

BOY: Don't you want to share?

ME: Oh, okay.

Drink arrives.

BOY: Like this.

Sticks straws in.

One for me and one for you.

ME: Oh, kay. Funny.

They drink.

BOY: Lick.

ME: Lickey.

BOY: Lick.

ME: Lickey.

BOY: Lick.

ME: *To the audience:* He just licked me. Flicked me with his tongue.

BOY: Raspberry.

ME: Top lip.

BOY: Lime.

ME: Bottom lip.

BOY: Lickey.

ME: Tongue.

BOY: Tongue.

ME: Thick, poking.

BOY: Rise, blood, filling, filling.

ME: Poke.

BOY: Wanting, wanting.

ME: Poke. Poke.

BOY: Wanting!!!!!!!

ME: I don't get it.

BOY: See you.

ME: Yeah, okay.

BOY *hooks up with someone else.*

I have always liked being by myself, have always had things to do, so I guess that's a good thing since I don't really like anyone half as much as everyone else seems to . . .

Spoken with a very loaded tone:

. . . like each other.

A new girl approaches. She has not been part of the crowd.

GIRL: You see the maple?

ME: Yeah.

GIRL: The one behind the field, down the path.

ME: Past the bog.

GIRL: Near the rock.

ME: That's my rock.

GIRL: That's my tree.

ME: You have a tree?

GIRL: You have a rock?

ME: Sometimes a tree.

GIRL: Sometimes a rock.

ME: Since I could walk.

GIRL: Since I could crawl.

ME: Since I was born.

GIRL: Since forever.

ME: I used to leave my ma's womb at night to go sit on my rock.

GIRL: I waited in that tree till my folks fucked to make me.

ME: I'm . . . out. . . .

GIRL: I'll show you my tree if you show me your rock.

ME: Okay.

GIRL: Now?

ME: Now. Yeah.

GIRL: Come on.

ME *and* GIRL *walk away from the school yard down the path.*

ME: Butterflies.

GIRL: Wonder.

ME: Something. Something. Something.

GIRL: Hurry.

ME: Last one.

GIRL: Last one.

ME: Racing.

GIRL: Breath.

ME: Heart.

GIRL: Beat.

ME: Beating.

GIRL: I like this rock.

ME: I like this tree.

GIRL: There's only one thing wrong.

ME: You have to go home?

GIRL: I'm eighteen.

ME: I know.

GIRL: Eighteen-year-olds don't have to . . . anything.

ME: I have to a lot of things.

GIRL: I know.

ME: Then what's wrong?

GIRL: You're over there.

ME: You're over there.

GIRL: Tree or rock?

ME: Tree.

GIRL: Here I come.

ME: Okay.

GIRL: Quick.

ME: Lips.

GIRL: Tongue.

ME: Luscious. I didn't know I knew that word, I didn't know, I didn't know.

GIRL: Luscious.

ME: More.

GIRL: Sweet.

ME: More.

GIRL: Salt.

ME: More.

GIRL: Yummy.

ME: You.

GIRL: You.

ME: Stay.

GIRL: Stay.

ME: Stay. I get it.

 Out.

I get it.

 Back to GIRL.

I get it.

END OF PLAY

SHE CAME IN THROUGH THE BATHROOM WINDOW

Tira Palmquist

She Came in Through the Bathroom Window was first performed in 2013 at the Orange County School of the Arts in an evening of faculty-written plays. It was directed by Cecelia Hamilton and Agnes Nguyen and performed by the following cast:

HILLARY: Ellen Webre
JULES: Jaide Mandas

CHARACTERS

HILLARY: *a 16-year-old young woman who really ought to think twice, even though she's plenty smart.*

JULES: *a 17-year-old young woman who if you think you know everything about her, you're probably wrong.*

TIME

After dark, a Friday night.

SETTING

A girls' bathroom in a high school.

> *Night. A girls' bathroom at a medium-size American high school. Light from a small window illuminates the sinks and stalls. It's quiet. Then, we hear the grunts of someone shoving something through an open window. A backpack, shoved through the window, thuds to the floor. Then, we see someone emerge through the opening and, clumsily, the someone also falls to the floor. This is HILLARY, a slightly geeky girl, dressed entirely in black, a kind of an attempt at a Mission: Impossible look. She pulls a headlamp out of her backpack, adjusts the headband around her forehead, and turns on the light. Then, the door to the bathroom opens, and another girl, moving with confidence and purpose, bumps smack into HILLARY, who falls backward, onto her butt. The new girl, dressed in urban chic tough-girl clothes, wearing boots and toting a retro-military messenger bag, is more surprised than anything.*

JULES: Hey . . .

HILLARY: Ow!

JULES *looks at* HILLARY*'s ridiculous outfit, and smirks.*

JULES: Whoa.

HILLARY: I'm sorry—I'm sorry . . .

JULES: *Squinting, from the glare of the headlamp.* Jesus. Turn that off, wouldja?

HILLARY *reaches up and turns off the lamp.*

HILLARY; Wait. Where'd you come from?

JULES: Uh . . . the hallway?

HILLARY: No. I mean "Where'd you come from" where'd you come from.

JULES: Yeah.

Looking again at HILLARY's *outfit.*

I could ask you the same question. You left the window wide open, FYI.

JULES steps to the mirror, to reapply some dramatic and dark lipstick.

HILLARY: You were following me, weren't you?

JULES: Hey. Maybe you were following me.

HILLARY: No—I've been planning this for weeks! I chose this bathroom because you can climb the tree out there and get in the window the easiest. And the front office is just down the hall—so I could do this as quick as possible. I made sure the window was unlocked . . .

JULES: Oh, I forgot: I don't care. *Beat.* Following you. Right.

JULES puts the finishing touches on her makeup.

HILLARY: Wait. I know you. You're that Julie girl in my . . .

JULES: Jules.

HILLARY: I thought your name was Julie.

JULES: I don't go by Julie. I go by Jules.

HILLARY: Oh. Okay. Well. You're that . . . Jules girl in my AP Lit class.

JULES turns to look at her. Then the recognition.

JULES: Ohhhhhh! Hillary Clinton!

HILLARY: Benson. It's Hillary Benson.

JULES: Jesus. Okay.

HILLARY: I hate it when people call me Hillary Clinton.

JULES: Well, I hate it when people call me Julie.

HILLARY: I guess we have something in common, then.

JULES: Trust me. We have nothing in common, okay?

A pause, while HILLARY *watches* JULES *applying more eyeliner. It's clear that* HILLARY *is stalling, waiting for* JULES *to go.*

JULES: Less than nothing. If it was possible to have negative things in common, that's what we'd have. Negative things in common.

Sees HILLARY *looking at her.*

JULES: Uh, don't let me keep you.

Beat.

HILLARY: I don't want you to see where I'm going.

JULES: Look. I really don't care where you're going. So just go, okay?

HILLARY *turns on her headlamp and goes for the door.*

See ya . . .

HILLARY *stops, turns off the headlamp.*

HILLARY: Oh, hold on. You can't tell anyone you saw me here. I can't get in trouble.

JULES: If you didn't want to get in trouble, you shouldn't have broken into school.

HILLARY: This is serious!

JULES: Jesus! Okay! *Beat.* I am totally curious now, though. What are you doing here? Stealing the SAT scores or something?

HILLARY: No! Just—you know—something for school.

JULES: Wearing that getup? I kinda doubt it. Lara Croft you are not.

HILLARY: I don't need a fashion critique, okay?

JULES: Fine. Go. *Beat.* After you tell me what you're doing.

JULES *steps in front of* HILLARY, *blocking her path.*

HILLARY: *A big, frustrated sigh.* It's . . . complicated.

JULES: You are getting more interesting by the minute. Wearing all black, breaking into school—this is golden.

HILLARY: It's not like anything you'd be doing.

JULES: Hey. Whoa. What the hell does that mean?

HILLARY: Nothing! *Beat.* Wait. What were you doing here?

JULES: Why?

HILLARY: If I get caught, I don't want to get blamed for something you did.

JULES: For something I did? What exactly do you imagine I was doing?

HILLARY: I don't know what you were doing.

JULES: That's not what I asked. I asked what you imagined I was doing—which is, apparently, pretty bad. I mean, just look at me. Right? I'm just the worst, right?

HILLARY: No, no—I obviously don't know anything about you. I'm sorry.

JULES: But you imagine all sorts of stuff. All sorts of nefarious goings on.

HILLARY: Well, I didn't imagine you knew the word "nefarious," for one thing.

JULES: Thus proving my point.

HILLARY: So—what were you doing?

JULES: Oh, terrible things. I was . . . spray painting terrible, terrible words on the walls of the vice principal's office. I let a terrible raccoon loose in the dance studio. And I set a terrible fire in the teachers' lounge. *Beat.* Happy?

HILLARY: No. I don't for a minute believe that you did any of those things.

JULES: But you imagined that I might have done something even worse?

HILLARY: Holy cats! I don't know! I don't know why anyone would break into school.

JULES: And yet here you are—breaking into school.

Coming close to her.

What's the story, Clinton?

HILLARY: Don't call me that!

JULES: Okay, Hillary. Someone this worried about getting in trouble must have a REALLY good reason for breaking in.

HILLARY: Oh, I do, but . . .

JULES: Come on. Tell me. Tell me. Tell me. Tell me.

HILLARY: Geez. Okay.

Big breath.

So. Do you know Jacob Goldman?

JULES: *Beat, thinking.* No.

HILLARY: He's in that band—the Salton Sea? He's in AP Lit with us? Dark curly hair?

JULES: Oh. Right. The dude who always carries his guitar around like any minute he's gonna be struck with musical inspiration. The broody one.

HILLARY: He's not broody. He's serious.

JULES: Okay. Whatever. So what is it about this Jacob "I think I'm Bob Dylan" Goldman of the Salton Sea that you find utterly charming and adorable?

HILLARY: Who's Bob Dylan?

JULES: Never mind. So what does Jacob "Dylan" Goldman have to do with breaking into school?

HILLARY: I'm asking him to Winter Formal.

> HILLARY *pulls a thumb drive out of the front pocket of her backpack. Beaming:*

I've taped my invitation here. I wrote a song, and recorded it, and I'm going to copy this into the files for Monday morning's school video announcements. At the end of it, I ask him to Winter Formal, and give him my number . . .

JULES: Whoa. Stop.

HILLARY: It'll be spectacular.

JULES: You cannot do this.

HILLARY: It's romantic!

JULES: It's—pathetic. And sad.

> *Holding out her hand.*

Give that to me.

HILLARY: It's not sad.

JULES: *Holding out her hand more forcefully.* Yeah, it totally is. You don't want to do this.

HILLARY: Go big or go home! You know? Haven't you ever seen *Say Anything . . .*?

JULES: Lloyd Dobler did not commit social suicide to win the heart of whatever her name was.

HILLARY: He would have appreciated the big romantic gesture.

JULES: He kept his big romantic gestures private. In her yard. Where no one else could see.

HILLARY: Why shouldn't everyone else see? I really like him. I want him to know that I went through a lot of trouble, that I really put thought into it.

JULES: He'll think you're crazy. And he would not be wrong.

HILLARY: Fine! Think I'm crazy! But I'm doing it!

HILLARY *tries to get to the door.* JULES *blocks her path.*

JULES: Nope. I'm not gonna let you do this.

HILLARY: Get out of my way—JULIE!

JULES: Oh, that's it, Clinton!

In a few quick moves, JULES *has* HILLARY *tackled, and in some kind of wrestling hold. This is a big and fairly ridiculous affair, with significant yelling and screeching.* JULES *has the upper hand, holding* HILLARY *down with one hand, and trying to wrench the thumb drive out of* HILLARY*'s fist with the other.*

JULES: Give it.

HILLARY: Stop that! Let go of me!

JULES: Get—your—grubby—fingers . . .

HILLARY: No!

JULES: Let. Go!

HILLARY: Forget it, Julie!

JULES *licks* HILLARY*'s hand, which grosses her out so much that she drops the thumb drive.* JULES *jumps up with the thumb drive, triumphant.*

HILLARY: Jules! Give it back!

JULES: No. You'll just do something public and ridiculous with it.

HILLARY: What if I—Hey: I know. Look. I'll just email it to him.

JULES: And then he forwards it to a friend, and before you know it, it's viral. *Beat.* Look, I think you're a giant dork, but I'm not going to let you do this.

HILLARY: But I really want him to go to Winter Formal with me!

JULES: Then do what any normal human being does. Ask him.

HILLARY: But then . . . I'd have to talk to him.

Beat.

JULES: Wait. You've never talked to him?

HILLARY: Well . . . no. *Beat.* He's really . . . broody.

JULES: Jesus. Sit down, wouldja? *Pause.* SIT!

Meekly, HILLARY *complies.* JULES *sits next to her.*

JULES: So. You like him.

She nods.

But you've never talked to him.

HILLARY: No.

JULES: Well, how do you even know you like him? I mean, what do you even know about him?

HILLARY: He likes music.

JULES: Obviously.

HILLARY: And he doesn't have many friends. And . . . he likes reading.

JULES: And?

HILLARY: And that's it.

JULES: You've got to be kidding. That's it? That's going to be the basis of a relationship?

HILLARY: I don't have any friends either. I like to read, too.

JULES: I like to read, too, and you're not asking me out! You've got to know a little more about a person before you haul off and embarrass yourself in public like this.

HILLARY: I'm desperate.

JULES: I see that. But listen. You've got to just talk to him. Monday: you go up to him in AP Lit and try to have a conversation with him.

HILLARY: No, I can't. That is just way too scary. I am not brave enough for that.

JULES: But you're brave enough to break into school? To make this public—and completely crazy—announcement that will make you a pariah?

HILLARY: But—he'll be looking right at me.

JULES: That is the point, isn't it? Hillary. You know I'm right. *Beat.* Hillary.

HILLARY: Okay. I'll do it.

HILLARY *holds her hand out for her thumb drive.*

JULES: Oh, if you think I'm giving this back to you, you're nuts.

HILLARY: You do know how computers work, right? It's on my computer at home.

JULES: Well, I'll be holding this hostage then. Post any of your nonsense videos, and I'll recut my own version of your love note and post it all over YouTube. And you never know what kind of thing I'll come up with, though you can imagine it will be terrifying.

After a moment:

HILLARY: Fine.

JULES: That's my girl. You'll see. My way is going to be a lot more satisfying. And safer. Your Future. You will thank me. *Beat.* Now, come on. We gotta get out of here before the janitor comes in here to clean.

HILLARY: They actually clean in here?

JULES: Once a week, whether it needs it or not.

JULES holds out her hand, and helps HILLARY *to her feet.*

JULES: Okay. Come on, Hillary Benson, let's get out of here.

She heads up to the window. HILLARY *follows her.*

HILLARY: You never did tell me what you were doing here.

JULES: Okay. Fine.

Pulls a thick book out of her messenger bag.

I had to get this.

HILLARY: You broke into school for a book?

Beat.

JULES: *Off* HILLARY*'s look.* Neil Stephenson? You'd break into school for Neil Stephenson, too.

Beat.

Don't tell anyone, okay?

HILLARY: Who would I tell about you? I never even saw you.

They smile.

JULES: That's what I thought.

HILLARY: Yeah. *Beat.* Thanks, Jules.

JULES: Thanks for what? I never saw you either. *Beat.* See you Monday, Benson.

And she's gone. HILLARY *takes off her headlamp, and takes her shoes out of her backpack.*

HILLARY: See you Monday, Jules.

Smiles.

Lights out.

END OF PLAY

SNO-GLOBE & THE BIG ZIP

Sharyn Rothstein

Sno-Globe & the Big Zip was originally produced as part of the 52nd Street Project's Don't Be Late! Plays About Time Festival in January of 2009. It was directed by Laura Konsin and performed by the following cast:

THE BIG ZIP: Jason Gil
SNO-GLOBE: Chloe Moore
EVIL HENCHMAN: Jason Hare

CHARACTERS

THE BIG ZIP: *a teenage superhero with the power to zip things together.*

SNO-GLOBE: *a teenage superhero with the power to encapsulate anyone or anything in a giant snow globe.*

An **EVIL HENCHMAN** *(or* **HENCHWOMAN***): he (or she) has no lines and eats a sandwich at the end of the play.*

NOTE: THE BIG ZIP *is a boy and* SNO-GLOBE *is a girl, but the casting can really be however you want it to be: you could cast the play with two girls, two guys, or switch it up and make* SNO-GLOBE *a boy and* BIG ZIP *a girl. Whatever works best for your company! The* EVIL HENCH-MAN *(or* HENCHWOMAN*) can be performed by the actor playing* BIG ZIP *or* SNO-GLOBE *in full, face-covering mask and cape.*

TIME
The present.

SETTING
Wherever evil lurks! (And SNO-GLOBE *can get cell-phone reception.)*

A NOTE ABOUT MUSIC: The show's songs can be sung to whatever musical composition you come up with. Have fun and be creative!

SCENE 1

> THE BIG ZIP, *a superhero with the power to zip things together, sits slumped on the floor, angry.* SNO-GLOBE, *a superhero with the power to encapsulate anyone or anything in a giant snow globe, runs onto the scene.*

SNO: Get ready for a blizzard! Sno is on the scene!

ZIP: You're late.

SNO: *Ignoring him.* C'mon bad guys, step right up! Let's see what damage you can do when you're shivering with frostbite!

She looks around.

Where's the bad guy?

ZIP: He left.

SNO: He left? Bad guys don't just "leave." That's why they're the bad guys.

ZIP: They leave if the Zip's in town. I zipped his feet to his forehead and rolled him straight into the McDonald's deep fryer.

SNO: Ugh.

She takes out her cellphone and starts texting a friend.

I've always thought you got the weirdest superpower. Zipping someone's skin together. It's gross.

ZIP: At least it's effective. Your superpower's the most idiotic thing I've ever heard of.

SNO: I capture villains inside snow globes! Not only is that a proven crime-fighting technique, it also makes gift giving easy. At least I don't turn bad guys into parkas.

ZIP: If you think my superpower's so lame, why don't you ever get here on time to help fight the bad guys? By the time you show up, I've already got everything under control.

SNO: Oh yeah, like that time you zipped yourself to the Teeth Chatterer?

ZIP: I was trying to wear him down! But his power proved stronger than mine . . .

He clatters his teeth very quickly to show what happened. Then he shakes off the terrible memory. ZIP grabs SNO's cell phone away from her.

SNO: Hey!

ZIP: Maybe if you'd shown up to that fight on time I wouldn't have become the only superhero with dentures.

She grabs the phone back.

SNO: I was making an entrance.

ZIP grabs the phone again.

ZIP: It's not an entrance if everyone else has already left!

SNO: I'm sorry my life's more interesting than yours. I've got stuff to do. I can't just drop everything whenever there's trouble.

ZIP: You're a superhero. The definition of superhero is someone who drops everything whenever there's trouble.

SNO: I'm nontraditional.

ZIP: You're late.

SNO: I am not late. I'm popular. And maybe if you had any friends besides Gravity Girl and The Rotten Egg you'd understand that showing up to kick a little supervillain butt is not always my top priority. I mean, give a superhero a break.

She puts out her hand, for the phone. ZIP *gives it to her.*

ZIP: I think we should stop working together.

SNO: What?

ZIP: I'm trying to single-handedly save the world from evil, and you're trying to attend every party on planet Earth.

SNO: Parties are important. How did we know the Groundhog Day Vampire was coming? I was at a party with my friend Glimmer, who heard from another one of my friends, Vanessa . . .

ZIP: The point is we can't be a crime-fighting superduo if you never show up until after the crime fighting is done.

SNO: You really mean it? We've been fighting villains together since kindergarten. And now you're done? Just cause I'm a little late sometimes?

ZIP: You always used to be right on time. But over the last couple of years . . . whenever I call you, you're like, "Yeah, yeah, yeah, super villain Whatever."

SNO: It's easier to find time to destroy bad guys when your life is afterschool snacks and *Spongebob Square Pants*. I've got social obligations now. Friends I want to spend time with.

ZIP: And I don't?

SNO *shrugs.*

SNO: Guess not.

ZIP *runs at her, about to turn her face into a zipper.*

ZIP: Why I oughta zip your lips to your earlobes!

SNO *throws a surge of icy wind at* ZIP.

SNO: You'd better watch it, or you're gonna spend the night in a glass bubble with a wind chill of below freezing and little plastic penguins dancing on your face!

ZIP *stops chasing her.*

ZIP: I'm sorry my life's not all about spreading rumors and going to cool parties.

SNO: I'm sorry my life's not at all about sitting alone in dank, dirty alleyways.

ZIP: That's where evil lurks!

SNO: How would you know? You've never looked anywhere else!

ZIP: This is exactly why we shouldn't work together anymore. You have no respect for the craft of super crime fighting!

SNO: I may have no respect, but you have NO LIFE!

ZIP and SNO turn their backs on each other and storm offstage.

SCENE 2

A peal of evil laughter. It's a couple of weeks later and ZIP is patrolling for bad guys, alone. He sings to himself.

ZIP: I don't need friends,

friends make you lonely,

I don't need help,

I can trust myself only.

Evil won't wait,

for a hero who's late,

who arrives at the end,

that's why . . .

That's why . . .

I don't need friends.

'Cause heroes don't need company,

Another peal of laughter. ZIP shivers. Unseen by ZIP, SNO takes the stage, patrolling as well. They sing together.

SNO: They're better off alone,

SNO/ZIP: When your power makes you

invincible,

you become completely

invisible

That why . . .

Heroes don't need company

ZIP *follows the laughter offstage.*

SNO: I don't take orders,

Spoken:

I give 'em.

I owe nobody nothin'—

that's livin'!

I like to have fun,

go out every night

'Cause life doesn't wait,

while you do what's right,

while you help defend . . .

That's why . . .

that's why . . .

I don't take orders, I give 'em!

 Another peal of evil laughter. SNO *shakes, scared.*

'Cause heroes don't need company,

They're better off alone,

When your power makes you

invincible,

you become completely

invisible

That why . . .

 Suddenly, from offstage, she hears ZIP.

ZIP: By the power of Zip, I command you to let me go!

 Then, meekly:

Please?

SNO: Zip?! Zip, I'm coming!

 SNO *runs offstage.*

SCENE 3

 SNO *and* ZIP *sit onstage, exhausted.*

ZIP: I had it all under control.

SNO: You had zipped your eyes closed.

ZIP: I couldn't watch.

SNO: It was brave of you to tackle the Angry Greenbean by yourself. He's ruthless.

ZIP: Whatever. I was just doing my job. This still doesn't mean we're partners, by the way.

SNO: I know. Please. I just had to save your sorry self. You think I want to go back to being partners?

ZIP: The only reason you had to save me was because I got there first. You were late, as always.

SNO: I wasn't late for anything. We don't work together anymore, remember? I can show up whenever I want. If I want to show up at all.

Pause. They look away from each other.

ZIP: So why'd you show up?

SNO: I don't know. I felt like it.

ZIP: Well . . . thanks.

They look at each other.

SNO: I'm sorry I said you didn't have any friends. Gravity Girl's really . . . got her feet on the ground. And the Rotten Egg . . . okay, I've got nothing good to say about the Rotten Egg. I just think if you loosened up a little maybe you'd be more fun to hang around with. Like you used to be.

ZIP: If I'm not fun anymore maybe it's because the world's a dark, frightening place and . . .

SNO: Yeah. It is. That's why it's not just enough to be a superhero. You need friends to make it less dark and frightening.

ZIP: I thought you were my friend.

SNO: Oh man, that is so sappy. See? Nobody wants to hang out with sappy superheroes. It's lame.

ZIP: Superman's sappy. AND he's on time. You know why he's on time? Because otherwise his motto would be: Look! In the sky, it's a bird, it's a plane, it's . . . it's . . . it's another bird.

SNO: You're not Superman! And the world doesn't need you to fight all of its supervillains all of the time.

ZIP: But if we're not here to fight them—

SNO: Then what? They'll probably go get a sandwich and wait for use to come find them. I mean, what's a supervillain without a superhero to fight?

ZIP: Just a regular villain I guess.

SNO: Exactly. You don't have to be here the minute they show up. Give them some time to wreak havoc first. Then you'll look like an even bigger hero.

ZIP: That's so irresponsible.

SNO: So what? We may be superheroes, but we're also teenagers. We're allowed to be a little irresponsible sometimes. Hey. I'm going to Sapphire's birthday party tonight. You can come but you can't do that thing you do when you get socially awkward and start zipping people to the furniture.

ZIP: As long as you don't put me in a snow globe when I'm trying to get to the bathroom.

SNO: I only did that once.

ZIP shoots her a look.

Twice.

He shoots her another look.

Eight times. But it was so funny! Okay, okay, I promise I won't do that anymore. So . . . are we still a crime-fighting duo?

ZIP: Are you going to try to show up on time, at least for the really bad bad guys?

SNO: Yeah. Are you gonna try to be more laid back, at least when it comes to petty thieves and minor henchmen?

ZIP: I'll try.

SNO throws her arm around ZIP's shoulder and sings.

SNO: Even heroes, they need company,

ZIP: No one's better off alone,

SNO/ZIP: When your power makes you

invincible,

you become

invisible

That why . . .

Heroes,

even heroes,

Heroes need

company.

SNO: Sno-Globe and The Big Zip: Crime-fighting in its awkward years.

ZIP: You mean The Big Zip and Sno-Globe.

SNO: No. I mean Sno-Globe and The Big Zip!

> *They head off together, bickering.*

> *An* EVIL HENCHMAN *(or* HENCHWOMAN*) sneaks in and gives a big, evil cackle. But there's no response. He cackles again. Nothing. He looks bored. He takes out a sandwich and starts to eat it.*

END OF PLAY

ZOMBIE RADIO

Don Nigro

CHARACTERS
MEREDITH CHERRY, *17*
JIM RAINEY, *18*

TIME
The autumn of the year 1954.

SETTING
A sofa in the living room of a brick house at 405 Armitage Avenue in Armitage, a small town in eastern Ohio.

> MEREDITH *and* JIM *are sitting on the sofa, facing downstage toward an invisible black-and-white television set. They are watching in the dark, with just the ghostly television light upon them. Muted sounds of an old horror movie on the invisible television set from time to time. What they are watching is a very old, early thirties horror movie.* MEREDITH *is cuddled under* JIM's *arm. It's late at night. She's babysitting. She's eating a peach.*

MEREDITH: Isn't this a great movie?

JIM: Are you kidding? This is the stupidest thing I've ever seen in my life. The people who aren't playing zombies are so bad they're more like zombies than the people playing zombies.

MEREDITH: It's remarkable how potent cheap music can be.

JIM: What?

MEREDITH: Noel Coward said that on the radio. He means that sometimes something that isn't actually made very well can still give you a lot of pleasure by creating a really powerful atmosphere you can get lost in.

JIM: I don't want to get lost. I want to watch something that makes sense, like football. Do you have to eat that damned peach? It's dripping all over the place. We've got popcorn and you're eating a peach.

MEREDITH: I was hungry for peaches. I've been getting all kinds of weird cravings lately. And sometimes I can smell bacon frying when nobody is cooking bacon. And also I've been hearing these radio broadcasts in my head. I mean, not real ones. It's like, there's this special frequency and I'm the only one tuned to it, and I can hear these voices and sounds and this music. It's just like murmuring in the background all the time, and sometimes somebody turns it up, and I can hear parts of it really clearly, and then it gets all garbled again.

JIM: What is it? Like Mars communicating with you? Is the mother ship calling you home?

MEREDITH: I don't think it's from Mars. I don't know where it's from. And I've been having a lot of nightmares, really disturbing ones, and I wake up in the middle of the night all sweaty and shaking so I go downstairs and open the refrigerator in the dark, because I like to see the light streaming out of the refrigerator into the darkness, like a picture of God in my old Bible storybook.

JIM: So you've been hearing voices and smelling bacon and you think God lives in your refrigerator?

MEREDITH: No, silly. Not just my refrigerator. Everybody's refrigerator. I mean, if God is everywhere, then he's in the refrigerator, right?

JIM: You think he's in the toilet, too?

MEREDITH: I think everywhere means everywhere. If you believe that sort of thing. I don't know if I do or not. But I keep getting this feeling there's things going on all around me that I don't quite understand. It's like I'm a radio and my reception isn't good enough to draw in everything that's zapping through the air, so I just get these fragments of dialogue, sudden bursts of revelation, like listening to the radio late at night. Which I do sometimes when I can't sleep and go downstairs and have an onion and anchovy sandwich at three in the morning, and maybe I don't want to go back to sleep, because I've been dreaming that rats are eating the baby or something. And also I keep losing everything. I lost my keys. I lost my driver's license. I lost the cat. Except that came back. I lost my virginity in the back seat of your Chevy during *The Creature from the Black Lagoon* at the drive-in. That's not coming back. Some things you can find again and some things, once you lose them, they're gone forever. And that's a long time. As we learn from popular songs on the radio. Also, I believe in ghosts.

JIM: There aren't any ghosts. That's almost as stupid as zombies.

MEREDITH: Well, it's not like Caspar the Friendly Ghost or people wearing sheets like in Three Stooges movies or anything like that. I mean I can feel these presences all around me. Like watching us.

JIM: Were they watching what we just did on the sofa?

MEREDITH: God, I hope not. Don't you ever get the feeling there's all kinds of presences around you, watching you?

JIM: No.

MEREDITH: You know why I liked you at first? Because you were so quiet. I figured that meant you were deep. But it turned out you just didn't have anything to say.

JIM: I've got plenty to say. I just don't feel like yapping all the time like you. Do they have any more beer?

MEREDITH: We can't drink all of Mr. Palestrina's beer. I'm the babysitter. I can't get drunk.

JIM: But you can screw me on the sofa.

MEREDITH: Oh, God, we shouldn't have done that. What if Ben came down and saw us? What if he heard something and came down the steps and was looking at us from the doorway while it was happening?

JIM: Then he's a pervert.

MEREDITH: He's not a pervert. He's a little boy.

JIM: He's weird.

MEREDITH: He's not weird. Well, he's a little bit weird. But I like it. He's a lot nicer to me than you are.

JIM: He just wants to see you naked.

MEREDITH: He's five years old.

JIM: I've seen the way that kid looks at you in your swimsuit. Trust me, he wants to see you naked.

MEREDITH: But you like children, right?

JIM: No, I don't. They're a pain in the ass.

MEREDITH: You wouldn't like to have children some day?

JIM: Nope.

MEREDITH: But you would, if we got married.

JIM: I don't want to get married.

MEREDITH: You mean right now, or ever? You don't want to be

alone for the rest of your life.

JIM: I'm not alone. You're here. Well, part of you is here. Most of you is usually someplace else, listening to the damned radio in your head.

MEREDITH: I'm not someplace else. Except sometimes I can almost remember being someplace else. Somebody else. Like before I was born.

JIM: What a bunch of crap that is.

MEREDITH: It's not crap. Ben told me he can almost remember being somebody else, in a previous life.

JIM: Ben is nuts, and so are you. You are the weirdest girl in this whole town. And this is a pretty weird town.

MEREDITH: I think you'd be good with children, if you had one. I mean, if we got married and had one.

JIM: If we got married and had a kid, I'd step in front of the nearest locomotive.

MEREDITH: You don't mean that.

JIM: How do you know what I mean?

MEREDITH: It could happen, you know. Girls do get pregnant. And then what can you do?

JIM: Hop on the next boxcar to Fresno.

MEREDITH: You wouldn't do that.

JIM: I'd rather be dead. Like those zombies in this stupid movie.

Pause. Sound of the movie.

MEREDITH: Do you think zombies eat babies?

JIM: I don't know what zombies eat. I got to go. Me and Cletis are going hunting tomorrow.

MEREDITH: I don't understand how you can take pleasure from killing things.

JIM: It's human nature. Kill or be killed. Law of the Jungle. Ask the voices you hear on the radio in your head. They'll tell you.

MEREDITH: I don't like killing things. *Pause.* Some people get rid of their babies before they're born. But I would never do that. I'd rather die.

JIM: *Getting up and starting to go.* Okay. See you later.

MEREDITH: *Trying to pull him back.* Wait. Don't you want to see the end of the movie?

JIM: I know the end of the movie. They kill the zombies. That's the end of the movie.

MEREDITH: Poor zombies. I feel sorry for them.

JIM: You feel sorry for zombies?

MEREDITH: Zombies are people, too.

JIM: You feel sorry for everything. You feel sorry for the chicken while you're eating it. You even felt sorry for the damned Creature from the Black Lagoon. All the time we were doing it in the back seat you were crying.

MEREDITH: Well, he was lonely.

JIM: He was a monster.

MEREDITH: He was just different. It's not a crime to be different. Or at least it shouldn't be.

JIM: Great. That's your perfect mate. Something with flippers and gills. You can have babies with him. Little frog-face babies. I hope you'll be very happy together.

MEREDITH: I want to tell you something.

JIM: Tell me later.

MEREDITH: I could be dead later.

JIM: Then you can come back as a zombie and tell me while you're eating the baby.

He goes. Pause.

MEREDITH: Yeah. Thanks a lot, Jim. You're a great listener. You're going to make a wonderful father some day.

Pause. She sits down, looks at the movie.

Watch out, zombies. They're coming to get you. I wonder if zombies hear voices in their heads. I bet they do. They always look like they're listening to something we can't hear. Maybe it's better to be dead. Or live at the bottom of a lagoon.

Pause. Faint sound of the movie. She's listening to something else.

What? Speak up. I can almost make it out. Like somebody is trying to tell me something. What are you trying to tell me? What should I do? Tell me what to do. Please tell me what to do.

Sound of a faint screaming from inside the television set. The light fades on her and goes out.

END OF PLAY

Plays for Middle Schools

BAND GEEKS

Kayla Cagan

CHARACTERS
RYAN: *12*
JOSH: *14*
ZAC: *16*
The three boys are The Chimsky Brothers.

TIME
Fall—the beginning of the school year.

SETTING
The Chimsky living room, in Chicago, Illinois.

> RYAN, JOSH, *and* ZAC *are all hanging out in their living room.*
> RYAN *is playing a video game on his Xbox,* JOSH *is laying across the couch reading a magazine,* ZAC *sits in the big lazy chair, strumming his guitar. They are quiet for a while, not really paying attention to each other.*

ZAC: I've been thinkin'. . .

JOSH: *Laughing.* Oh no, not that again! Don't strain yourself!

> *RYAN laughs.*

ZAC: Whatever.

RYAN: Oh no, Josh! You made him stop thinking!

> RYAN *snickers.*

ZAC: You twerp! Both of you—dorks!

JOSH: *Sing-songy.* Dork, york, jork . . .

> ZAC *looks exhausted with them.*

What? What?

RYAN: Stop, you're going to make him think again!

> *Both* RYAN *and* JOSH *crack up.*

ZAC: Go 'head . . . you . . . you idiots. You wouldn't even understand anyway. Never mind.

RYAN: What? What wouldn't I get?

> *Paying attention to his video game, he just lost one of his men.*

AW, MAN!!!

JOSH: Yo! You killed Zoron!

RYAN: No, I didn't—he killed me! I'll get him back!

He is focused back on the game.

ZAC: See, you two are like Dumb and Dumber. I knew you wouldn't get it!

JOSH: Get what?

RYAN: Just say it, Dork-us!

JOSH: I bet I know what it is.

ZAC: What?

JOSH: *Sing-songy.* Zac's got a girlfriend, Zac's got a girlfriend, you like Re-bec-ca, you like Re-bec-ca . . .

ZAC: No, I don't!

RYAN: *Sing-songy.* You're gonna kiss her, you're gonna kiss her!

ZAC: Oh, arg! I live with the two most stupid morons on earth! I don't even know how we're related . . .

RYAN: Well, duh, we're related through Mom and Dad, Sir Dorks-a-lot. Need me to explain?

ZAC: Never mind. I don't know why I thought I could share any ideas with you two in the first place. I'm outta here!

He starts to leave the room.

JOSH: No, wait!

RYAN: Just kidding, man!

JOSH: Take a joke!

RYAN: We don't care if you like Re-bec-ca!

ZAC: Well, I don't for your information. She's just my friend. And she's not what I was thinking about.

RYAN: Well?

JOSH: (We're) . . . Waiting, dude!

ZAC picks at his guitar.

ZAC: Band.

JOSH and RYAN: What? Huh?

ZAC: I'm starting a band. *Pause.* And I'm going to quit marching band.

JOSH: What?

RYAN: You're going to be in so much trouble!

JOSH: What about your drums? And your uniform and everything?

ZAC: *Raising an eyebrow.* Oh, I'll still practice my drums. . . . Um . . . my uniform . . .

RYAN: Mom and Dad are never going to let you quit!

JOSH: They'll kill you!

ZAC: They won't kill me.

RYAN: Uh-huh.

JOSH: Yes, they will!

ZAC: No, they won't—because I'm not going to tell them.

RYAN: What?

JOSH: Are you crazy?

RYAN: You'll never get away with it.

ZAC: Watch me. And you two . . .

JOSH: What?

RYAN: Don't look at me! I just got out of trouble!

Another one of his men dies. He stops the game for a moment.

Ah man!

ZAC: Listen, I'm not going to be some one-man-band. I'm going to need some help.

Turning to JOSH.

You don't want to be in band forever, do you?

JOSH: Well, I . . .

ZAC: All you do is complain about formations! Imagine playing without being told what you have to do, how you have to march! You're a good enough saxophonist—they can't teach you to be better, only practice makes you better!

JOSH: So?

ZAC: So, you'll practice with me.

JOSH: What? When?

ZAC: After school, the same time we usually have practice.

JOSH: But that's when we have band!

ZAC: Exactly.

He lets the double meaning sink in to JOSH.

I can finally start singing, for real. I'll play the guitar too. You can be on sax and we'll get Mike Dody on drums.

RYAN: He's mean. And his sister stinks.

ZAC: Maybe so. But he's an awesome drummer.

JOSH: Yeah, and nobody said you were in it anyway!

ZAC *smiles.*

ZAC: So, you're in?

Pause.

JOSH: I'm in.

RYAN: So am I.

ZAC: What?

RYAN: I'm in too.

ZAC: Uh, no you aren't. You're too young.

RYAN: Bull!

ZAC: You wouldn't get it.

JOSH: Yeah!

RYAN: Yes, I would! I'm. In. The. Band.

ZAC: No. You. Aren't. You can help out if you want. You'll be like our roadie. Help us keep it quiet for a while from Mom and Dad.

RYAN: Nope. I'm in the band. If Josh's in, I'm in.

JOSH: But you don't even like your piano lessons.

RYAN: So? I do now. I didn't like them. But now I do.

ZAC: Listen, Ryan . . .

RYAN: No! You can't talk me out of it!

ZAC: You aren't in the band.

RYAN: Yes. I. Am. Or else.

ZAC: Or else what?

RYAN: Or else I tell Mom and Dad everything.

ZAC: You wouldn't!

RYAN: Try me.

JOSH: You're just being a baby because Z didn't ask you first!

RYAN: I am not.

JOSH: Are too!

ZAC: I can't believe this.

RYAN: So, do we have a deal?

ZAC: No, we don't have a deal.

RYAN: Either you agree that I play piano for the band or I tell. It's your choice.

JOSH: You little brat!

RYAN: What's it gonna be?

ZAC: Are you willing to practice?

RYAN: Yeah.

ZAC: And you can't complain about practice. If you complain even once, you're out. That's the rule.

JOSH: Do I get to complain?

ZAC: Nobody gets to complain. This is my band, get it? I'm the one who thought of it, I'm the one who is getting it together, I'm the one in charge. And I'm the lead singer. Agreed?

JOSH: Cool.

RYAN: That works for me.

ZAC: *Sarcastic.* Oh, good, I wouldn't want his royal dork-i-ness to go cry to Mom and Dad.

RYAN: When do we start?

ZAC: Next Monday, after school. I have to talk to Mike and make sure he's in.

JOSH: And what's our name?

ZAC: Good question. I haven't even thought of it yet.

RYAN: Let's be the Undercover Rockers.

JOSH: That's stupid.

RYAN: Do you have something better?

JOSH: How 'bout The Chimsky Brothers?

ZAC: No, 'cause Mike might be in the band. . . . I was thinking maybe something about the marching band.

RYAN: Drumline?

JOSH: No. Formation?

RYAN: Boring. You might as well call it Geometry.

ZAC: I don't know . . . everything about the band is so nerdy and we have to be cool.

RYAN: What about Cool School?

ZAC: I don't like it. But that's on the right track . . .

JOSH: Wait a minute . . . if marching band is nerdy, then what are the people in the band called? Band Geeks.

RYAN: Yeah . . .

JOSH: That's it! We are band geeks, but we're geeks for our own band, not somebody else's band!

ZAC: You want our name to be Band Geeks?

JOSH: I kind of like it.

ZAC: It does have a ring to it.

Into it.

Band Geeks . . .

JOSH: It works, doesn't it?

RYAN: We're gonna be nerds!

ZAC: So? We we're nerds in marching band, too. But this is our own band, our own brand of geek. We can do this. Are you in?

JOSH: In!

RYAN: In!

ZAC: Then, let's do this. Let the Band Geeks rule!

They strike rock-star poses.

Ladies and Gentlemen, live in the Chimsky freakin' living room, I give you the one . . .

ZAC grabs his guitar.

. . . the only . . .

RYAN *pretends to play the keyboards.*

. . . the amazing . . .

JOSH *pretends he is on his horn.*

. . . Band Geeks!!!!

Blackout as music blares.

END OF PLAY

THE CELL PHONE EPIDEMIC

Claudia Haas

CHARACTERS

JESS: *15; female; a chronic cell-phone user.*
ALICIA: *15; female; a self-absorbed but equally chronic cell-phone user.*

TIME

Today.

SETTING

Emergency waiting room in a hospital.

> JESS *is in an emergency room with a bandaged nose, impatient and embarrassed.*

JESS: I know! All right? I'll just wait here. I won't move. I won't text anyone! What would I say?

> *We hear someone yelling offstage.*

VOICE: *From offstage.* Yes, I called my mother! . . . I have insurance! I don't see why you can't help me right away! I mean look at me!

> ALICIA *enters. She is a mess—scraped and bruised and totally disheveled.*

JESS: Alicia?

ALICIA: Jess?

JESS and ALICIA: What happened to you?

ALICIA: Don't ask!

JESS: You look . . .

ALICIA: Disgusting—I know. And the police who brought me here—do you know what they did? They snickered! That's right! They seriously snickered! They were laughing at me during the whole ride to the hospital.

JESS: You . . . smell.

ALICIA: I know.

JESS: . . . really bad.

ALICIA: I know! Can we move on to another subject?

JESS: Can't . . . you clean yourself up or something?

ALICIA: No. I was told the doctor needed to see me "as is" first.

How lame is that? I mean, what if someone important—like a guy—sees me like this? I'd die. That's it! End of the world. Throw myself into the volcano and bid farewell to this so-called life!

JESS *moves away.*

JESS: What . . . happened?

ALICIA *moves in.*

Don't come any closer! You can tell me from there.

ALICIA: Nothing.

JESS: If you say so.

ALICIA: I fell.

JESS: Sorry.

ALICIA: Into a manhole.

JESS: Ouch!

ALICIA: Filled with sewage.

JESS: Gross me out!

ALICIA: And waterbugs . . . and roaches . . .

JESS: Rats?

ALICIA: RATS! Totally forgot about the rats! I'm going to be sick.

JESS: Well, you're in the right place for that!

ALICIA: I'm gross enough—I don't need to add to my misery!

JESS: Weren't there—like warning signs or something around the manhole?

ALICIA: No! It was totally open! They didn't have a sign! No cones! No flashing lights! I walk down Elm Street every day and there's never been a gaping hole in the middle of the street before. Why would I expect one now?

JESS: That is so irresponsible of the city!

ALICIA: I know! Tell me about it!

JESS: You should sue.

ALICIA: Most definitely. My mom she says she'll look into suing the city, the energy people, and anybody else a lawyer could find!

JESS: At least it would cover your medical bills.

ALICIA: And my mental "pain and suffering" from being underground with—gross stuff! And we're totally suing the police department for snickering at me in the squad car. That's what's great about this country: Land of the red, white, and sue, sue, sue!

JESS: They all seriously deserve it. For not doing their job. I'm sure it's covered under negligence—or something.

ALICIA: I know! I would've seen an orange cone while looking down on my phone. And if they were really responsible, they would have posted a guard to let people know the manhole was open!

JESS: You were texting?

ALICIA: Well, duh. Walking is so boring!

JESS: It's the worst! I was walking and before you know it—this lamppost jumped in front of me. That's how I broke my nose.

ALICIA: The streets are not safe anymore.

JESS: Tell me about it—there should be warning signs around lampposts.

ALICIA: That's what I'm saying. The city should totally have had a guard or something! For my protection! It's enough we have to deal with—you know—trees.

JESS: And curbs. Grace fell off the curb and broke her foot.

ALICIA: And then there's all those cracks in the sidewalks. . . .

JESS: . . . trash cans . . .

ALICIA: . . . . Stop signs . . .

JESS: It's like a minefield out there!

ALICIA: Sheesh! Don't people understand that there's a new world of cell phones and you can't always be looking straight ahead at the same old thing every day? It's not 1990 anymore. Cities have to grow and change and adapt to the way things are!

JESS: Do you know there are streets in London where they've put rubber cushioning on the lampposts because of all the accidents? London really cares for its citizens.

ALICIA: We should start a movement here!

JESS: We should! We can start a call-in to all the talk shows . . .

ALICIA: And post stuff on Facebook and Twitter—this could get big.

JESS: Wow, Alicia—this movement could make us famous!

ALICIA: And maybe we should picket manholes!

JESS: And organize something at school!

ALICIA: Except that—nobody really listens to a kid.

JESS: When we're grown, we'll change things. We'll make it so people can walk and text at the same time!

ALICIA: For sure. Of course, when we're grown we won't be walking anymore.

JESS: We'll have wheels!

ALICIA: I can't wait! Driver's license—here I come!

JESS: Your cell working?

ALICIA: Yes. No thanks to the city! It got scraped on the way down. Oh! Got a text! From Lizzy—she wants to know how I am—that's so sweet.

JESS: I'm going to see what Leah's doing.

> ALICIA *and* JESS *text.*

MOTHER'S VOICE: *From offstage.* Come on, Jess! Paperwork's done and I need to pick up your brother.

JESS: *Without looking up.* See ya—hope everything turns out okay.

ALICIA: Yeah, thanks. You, too.

> JESS *walks off texting while* ALICIA *continues to send messages on her phone.* JESS *bumps into something as she exits.*

JESS: *From offstage.* Owwww!

> *Blackout.*

END OF PLAY

OENONE

Ashley Cowan

CHARACTERS

OENONE: *12, a fairly average middle-school girl. She's at that stage where you know she'll grow up to be pretty but she's not quite there yet and can be a bit self-conscious about it. The one thing she's got going for her in this cruel world is a boyfriend, because having one allows her to pretend she has a higher status.*

HEATHER B: *12, a bit reserved. She's an easy target for harsh middle-school words. She is a true teacher's pet who is longing to be accepted by her friends and frenemies.*

TIFFANY: *13, a confident and effortlessly cool girl. She is tech savvy and is someone who somehow lucked out by not ever needing braces.*

TIME

The present.

SETTING

Study hall in a middle school.

NOTE: The story and characters are inspired by the Greek myth about Oenone and her influence on the Trojan War.

> *Lights up on three girls. They sit casually at a table inside the library—a little too casually considering they're not at a sleepover. It's study hall. After lunch, before gym class. In middle school. The second to last period of the day. In the air, a cloud of unappreciated angst lingers. Sprawled on the table are packets of Fun Dip, Starbursts, lip gloss, notebook papers, and their cell phones.*

HEATHER B: *Finishing a game of MASH.* Okay, Oenone. It says you're going to live in a mansion, marry Paris, drive a Volkswagen Beetle, and have one kid.

OENONE: Sounds right to me!

TIFFANY: How do you always get that fortune?

OENONE: Don't question the fates, Tiffany.

HEATHER B: Can I go next?

OENONE: I'm bored of MASH. Hey, did you guys watch *The Bachelor* last night?

HEATHER B: I'm not allowed to. My parents think it's trashy. And that it promotes an unhealthy notion that women can only find happiness when they're pitted against each other in a war to earn the love of one man.

TIFFANY: It's sooooo good. I can't believe he sent that redheaded one home. She was so skinny. But he probably did it because she was always crying about stuff.

HEATHER B: What kind of stuff?

OENONE: You'll understand when you get a boyfriend. Now it's just down to those two girls. The nice one and the mean one who is "not there to make friends." But it's so unrealistic that he's "in love" with both of them. Don't you think? I'm SO glad I'll never be on that show. Oh, can I get one of those, Heather B?

HEATHER B: *Sharing the Starburst candy.* You can just call me Heather if you want. Since I'm the only Heather here.

OENONE: I know. I'm just used to it.

TIFFANY: If you can unwrap a Starburst in your mouth without using your hands it means you're a good kisser.

HEATHER B: No way. That's impossible.

TIFFANY: It's the only real way to know for sure. Heather Q told me.

> *The girls all nod. Heather Q is a reliable source. They stare at the Starburst silently mocking them from the table. Each scared to reveal their true kissing skills.*

OENONE: Can I get some Fun Dip?

TIFFANY: That'll give you a sugar high for gym.

OENONE: Ew, I forgot we had gym next.

HEATHER B: We're playing indoor volleyball today.

OENONE: Ew. Do we still have to change clothes?

TIFFANY: Probably.

OENONE: Heather B, you're not wearing shorts are you?

HEATHER B: No . . .

OENONE: I just don't want people making fun of you again. I still don't get why you can't shave your legs.

HEATHER B: My mom won't let me.

OENONE: Your leg hair is so dark. *Beat.* But I think that color you're wearing looks good for your skin.

HEATHER B: What's wrong with my skin?

OENONE: Nothing! *Beat.* It's kind of pale.

HEATHER B: My orthodontist says it's pretty.

OENONE: Okay.

She returns to eating her Fun Dip.

TIFFANY: That is turning your tongue blue!

OENONE: Ew, really? Gross! Let me see. Do you have that mirror app on your phone?

TIFFANY: Obvi.

She glances at her phone, looks horrified, scrolls through some things, nervously peeks at OENONE, *and then looks to* HEATHER B *as if to say, "Yo, girl, pick up your phone and check this out!"* HEATHER B, *being the mind reader that all middle-school girls are, immediately understands and looks at her phone. She too looks completely appalled. And a little terrified.*

HEATHER B: *Staring at* OENONE *and shouting.* It's nothing!

OENONE: What? What's up?

HEATHER B: Um . . .

She looks for help but TIFFANY *is completely mesmerized by her phone.*

OENONE: What's going on? Is something on my face? *Whispering.* Do I need to pluck my eyebrows?

This finally breaks TIFFANY *and the girls stare at* OENONE, *not sure what to say.*

TIFFANY: I told you he was a bad idea, Oenone.

OENONE: Who? *Beat.* Paris? *Beat.* No. Tell me what's going on!

HEATHER B: I don't want to tell you, because I don't want to hurt your feelings. But I feel like I should tell you because I think you'd want to know and I LYLAS you.

OENONE: Just tell me!

TIFFANY: *Bringing her phone around.* Okay, look at his Facebook page. First: this check-in.

OENONE: Sparta Middle School? What is he talking about? It must be a joke. Or someone hacked his account.

TIFFANY: There's more.

OENONE: It's just a bunch of emoticons.

TIFFANY: *Very seriously.* Yeah. It's a heart. And a wink face. And the smile with the tongue sticking out.

HEATHER B: *Whispering intensely.* Ewwww.

OENONE: Maybe someone is Catfishing with his profile . . .

TIFFANY: No, there's his picture. Look at that selfie on Instagram! He tots used the Hudson filter.

HEATHER B: So cold . . .

OENONE: Whoa, whoa—who is that?

HEATHER B: The tag says "HottieHelen." She looks like a high schooler! I bet her mom lets her take Zumba . . .

TIFFANY: There's another one! In X-Pro II. He's kissing her cheek! And he commented, "literally the hottest grl in the world . . .

HEATHER B: *Trying to make a joke.* What, does she have a temperature of 110 degrees? And he spelled "girl" wrong!

TIFFANY: . . . hashtag, so blessed."

OENONE: What? No! *Beat.* Is this because he hates my bangs? I'm growing them out . . .

HEATHER B: Oenone, no, your bangs are beautiful.

> TIFFANY *shoots* HEATHER B *a glance.* OENONE's *bangs are not beautiful. But in the cruel, cruel world of middle school, it was a nice thing to say.*

If he can't see how great you are, he's missing out. He's a loser.

OENONE: No, he's not!

HEATHER B: Well, that's what my mom says about boys our age.

OENONE: You're just jealous because you don't have a boyfriend. You don't know what it feels like.

> *She starts to weep on the table and continues eating Starbursts while dipping her Fun Dip.*

HEATHER B: Do you want to go in the bathroom and sing some Taylor Swift?

OENONE: No!

HEATHER B: Oh. Some Adele, then?

OENONE: Show me Helen's Facebook page.

HEATHER B: Are you sure?

OENONE: Let me see it, Tiffany.

TIFFANY: Here it is. Whoa, look—she just went from "in a relationship" to "it's complicated" with some guy named Menelaus. Oh, and he seems really angry about these pictures with Paris!

She continues to scroll down on her phone.

Yeah, it looks like everyone at SMS wants to kill him.

HEATHER B: Whoa! The language they're using! We should flag this as inappropriate.

OENONE: What? Is he okay?

TIFFANY: Helen just tweeted that someone named Aphrodite is giving them a ride to the Denny's in Troy.

HEATHER B: What?! They know someone who can drive? That seems unsafe. And what, they are just leaving school early—

OENONE: Hold on. They're going to Denny's? He wouldn't—I mean, that's OUR special thing. We ALWAYS get milkshakes and split the Grand Slamwich and the Bacon Slamburger!

TIFFANY: Uh-oh. I think Menelaus is going to try and find them. It looks like he and some of his soccer team are trying to figure out how to get there.

HEATHER B: They are leaving school too? We should try and tell someone's parents.

OENONE: I can't believe he would do this to me! I thought he loved me! *Beat.* This means war!

She whips out her phone in a rage, ready for battle!

HEATHER B: What are you going to do?

TIFFANY: She posted this terrible picture of him with some ugly stuffed animal! Ugh. Why does he look like that . . .

HEATHER B: Oenone, you didn't!

OENONE: That's Cory. The stuffed animal he gave me for helping him with science homework. He begged me to delete this picture, but if he's going to humiliate me I'm going to post it!

TIFFANY: You also included a link with directions on how to get to Denny's? Interesting choice.

HEATHER B: Your picture is getting a lot of comments and shares, Oenone.

More to herself:

Isn't anyone in class?

OENONE: Good!

She checks her phone.

Paris! Oh, now, you text me?! He's asking me to help him out and take down the picture. Never!

She gets another text.

He says he's in a lot of trouble and he's scared! Well, he deserves it!

She texts back.

I'm going to text him that I'm never helping him with homework again!

TIFFANY: Whoa.

OENONE: Yeah! And his parents said they were going to take away his phone if he didn't pass his next test!

TIFFANY: I'd die.

She sees that OENONE *has gotten another text.*

What is it?

OENONE: He just texted that he's sorry. I'll never ever have another boyfriend!

She goes off into another world consumed in her own downward spiral of sadness, remorse, and anguish.

TIFFANY: *Checks her phone.* Looks like your directions helped. Helen just posted a picture of Menelaus at Denny's saying, "I didn't order this, hashtag, burger with, hashtag, awkward sauce. LOL. But for realz, I'm, hastag, scared!"

OENONE *wails a bit.*

HEATHER B: Guys. We need to calm down. Who wants to play a quick game of MASH?

TIFFANY: OMG. Paris deleted his Facebook account! Ew.

HEATHER B: Are you sure he didn't just make it private or something?

TIFFANY: What are you doing, Oenone?

OENONE: *Dramatically narrates what she types into her phone.* Well, I guess this is the hashtag, end. Hashtag, good-bye. Hashtag, forever.

She starts to take a selfie of herself looking sad.

Do my bangs look okay?

TIFFANY *kind of shrugs and* OENONE *gets a shot of herself; she looks at it and decides she doesn't like it. She adjusts her angle and pouts back at the phone again.*

HEATHER B: Don't you think you're being a little dramatic?

OENONE *glares a glare that could kill a sixth grader.*

TIFFANY: *To* HEATHER B *after looking over* OENONE*'s shoulder at the picture.* Let her filter it.

She notices that OENONE *is about to do something dangerous and crazy.*

No. No! You're seriously deleting your Facebook account too?! It's social suicide! Just because Paris got rid of his doesn't mean you need to go down in flames!

She looks at her phone.

You just texted me the flame emoticon.

HEATHER B: Oenone, are you okay? You haven't blinked in a while.

OENONE: *After she officially defies all reason and deletes her page, she dramatically throws her phone down into her bag.* Give me a Starburst.

HEATHER B *hands her a Starburst and* OENONE *puts it into her mouth. She unwraps it without her hands! She uses her teeth and stuff. The other girls are obviously amazed.*

HEATHER B: You did it. You're a good kisser.

OENONE *looks crazed.* HEATHER B, *sensing that this study hall has come to an end, quickly grabs all of their things.* OENONE *stands and fixes her bangs.* HEATHER B *and* TIFFANY *slowly stand behind her.*

OENONE: Now let's go to gym class.

END OF PLAY

THE PRESENT MIDNIGHT
Constance Congdon

CHARACTERS
ALICE: *16, a cynical girl.*
RANDALL: *13, ALICE's younger brother; he is not cynical.*

TIME
The present, midnight.

SETTING
On top of the pitched roof of a large, new house in a housing development, sometimes called "suburbs" even when there is no major city to be the urban center that the rows of streets and overpriced houses could be the "sub" to.

In the dark, we see ALICE siting on the roof, comfortably, in whatever clothes she found around her bed when she got dressed. She is barefoot. Her cell phone rings. She looks at it, decides not to take it, puts it down. It rings again, and she looks at it, takes the call.

ALICE: What.

Listens.

No.

She clicks off. After a beat, the cell phone rings again. She turns it off. She hears something, looks down (at the ground below—this would be the front yard of the house), then shouts at someone she sees down there.

DON'T YOU COME UP HERE!! DON'T . . .

But it's no use, the someone is going to come up. She prepares herself for the intrusion.

Why would I think I could have any privacy? Why?

She turns her phone back on and checks the battery power. Shouting down:

Bring my battery charger!

A couple of beats, then RANDALL enters, crawling, scooting toward her. He is dressed in his pajamas. He's wearing sneakers and has a flashlight in his mouth. It is on, the flashlight, so his cheeks are illuminated from the inside, making him look creepy or strangely beautiful, depending on whether you would be glad to see him, which ALICE is not.

Did you bring my battery charger?

RANDALL: No. I brought the flashlight.

ALICE: But I need the battery charger.

RANDALL: We need the flashlight more.

ALICE: My cell phone is going dead.

RANDALL: Who do you want to call?

ALICE: Good point. Neither of us have any friends since we moved to this place. A few months go by and everybody's gone.

RANDALL: I've got my cell phone.

ALICE: Never mind. Lisa is the only one and she's not home.

She turns her cell phone off.

RANDALL: You can use my cell phone.

ALICE: I don't want to use your crappy cell phone!! It's been god knows where. Didn't you drop it in the toilet at school?

RANDALL: That was that kid. Lacrosse team captain.

ALICE: I hardly think he was captain.

RANDALL: He made me call him "captain."

ALICE: Jeez!! You are such a wimp!

RANDALL: Don't call me that. Dad calls me that, too. I don't care.

Silence, listens for the parents fighting.

ALICE: Have you been crying?

RANDALL: Allergies.

He listens.

Uh-oh. They're quiet. They're going to notice we're gone.

ALICE: I don't care.

RANDALL: Of course, you do.

ALICE: Nope.

RANDALL: Well, I care.

ALICE: Wuss.

RANDALL: What if they use the ladder to come up here?

ALICE: Why would they want to come up here?

RANDALL: Because they'll worry about us?

ALICE: When, exactly, would that start? Them worrying about us? Before or after the Big Fight? Or the fight before that? Or the Mother of All Arguments about buying this too-big house that still smells new in that creepy way with chemicals that will probably kill us and whose fault was it that they bought this house?

RANDALL: They bought this house for us.

ALICE: They bought the house for YOU. They've given up on me.

RANDALL: No, they haven't.

ALICE: Case in point. I've been up here for quite a while and has anyone, other than you, come looking for me?

RANDALL: They're busy.

Beat.

ALICE: Parents don't have to like their children. I read an article about it on the Net.

RANDALL: They . . .

ALICE: Yeah? MMMMMMM?

RANDALL: THEY BOUGHT THIS HOUSE FOR US!!

ALICE: You. And now you're flunking whatever that is. I heard them talking.

RANDALL: Oh God.

Sound down below.

Shoosh.

ALICE: What?

RANDALL: I thought I heard something.

ALICE *looks down at the "yard."*

Be careful.

ALICE: I've been up here for hours. I know what I'm doing.

She sees something.

I think it's Dad.

RANDALL: What's he doing?

ALICE: I can't tell.

RANDALL: Has he found the ladder?

ALICE: As if . . .

RANDALL: I can't see him anymore.

ALICE: You're too close to the edge.

RANDALL: "As if" what?

ALICE: As if he would care enough to come up the ladder and see about us.

RANDALL: I would worry about him.

ALICE: Worry? Why?

RANDALL: Because he's been drinking and he might fall.

ALICE: You are too good.

RANDALL: Good for what? I totally flunked precalc.

ALICE: Why are you taking that, anyway?

RANDALL: I'm supposed to be premed.

ALICE: You are thirteen years old! How can you be pre—anything???

RANDALL: Mom thinks . . .

ALICE: Mom "thinks?" Mom doesn't think, Randy. She just does stuff. A lot of stuff. At a very fast rate. I think she's ADD.

RANDALL: "ADD?" Adults can't have ADD.

ALICE: Why not?

RANDALL: Because you grow out of it.

ALICE: No, the world just gets bored with you having it. It doesn't go away. And you take too much Adderall . . .

RANDALL: Ritalin.

ALICE: I'm pretty sure it's Adderall.

RANDALL: Ritalin.

ALICE: Which one is the upper?

RANDALL: You take the upper for being too up is all I know.

ALICE: ADD isn't the same as hyperactivity. Right?

RANDALL: I don't know. All I know is that Nam Jin took one of those pills, whichever one makes you stay up, and he stayed up for fifteen hours reading about mollusks and now he knows everything about mollusks. I need some of that stuff. For precalc. I gotta talk to Nam Jin.

ALICE: Good luck. He's gone back to Korea.

RANDALL: Back to Korea? "Back to?" He's never been there. How do you know?

ALICE: I don't. I just said that. He's in that magnet school.

RANDALL: Stop. Just stop. If there was a magnet school, we wouldn't have had to move here. We could have stayed where we were and bussed to the magnet school. Mom and Dad moved us here for the school we're going to. It's supposed to be the best.

ALICE: It's a crappy school.

RANDALL: No, it's not. It's the only thing about this neighborhood I like.

ALICE: Neighborhood? Where are the neighbors? Look. Do you even see any lights on? Anywhere?

RANDALL: A lot of the houses aren't sold yet. That's why.

Beat.

You've been up here for hours. Don't you have to pee?

ALICE: You crawl into that dormer on the other side of the roof. The window is unlocked.

RANDALL: I thought those were just decorative, those whatever you call them.

ALICE: "Dormers." You haven't been up there? You haven't wandered up there to see what they were?

RANDALL: I thought they were fake. They still have the stickers on the windows.

ALICE: What have you been doing, Randall?

RANDALL: I've been studying!! Trying to keep up!!

ALICE: You have to be careful because the flooring is just to cover up the insulation stuff and you come to the end and there's a little stair thingie that opens AND LOWERS when you step on it . . .

RANDALL: No way!!

ALICE: And that takes you to the hall by the upstairs half-bath.

RANDALL: You've been cheating?? All the time you been up here, you been cheating.

ALICE: I would call it "surviving."

RANDALL: Okay. I don't have to go. I'm just checking.

ALICE: You're just scared to go.

RANDALL: I am not. I climbed up here on that ladder!

Shines the flashlight in the direction of the ladder.

No! The ladder's gone!! Holy crap, the ladder's gone!!

ALICE: We have the dormer.

RANDALL: But who took the ladder?? They know we're up here!!

ALICE: And . . .?

RANDALL: Now they KNOW: We. Are. Up. Here.

ALICE: And I still say, "And?"

RANDALL: They'll. . .We'll . . .

ALICE: What, Randall? They'll do. . .what? Come and get us? They can't BECAUSE THE LADDER IS GONE. Think about it.

Imitating, aloud, their father's thought processes.

"Ladder? Kids must be on the roof. What shall we do, as good parents? What? Oh, what? I know. We'll remove the ladder. That will fix the problem. Our children, our former babies we adored so much, will be stranded on the roof. That will show them. Good job—us. We are excellent parents. Oh, I'm getting sleepy from all this fighting. I say, Deborah, let's turn in. Yawn."

RANDALL: Our parents wouldn't do that!

ALICE: Witness: absence of ladder.

RANDALL: But . . .

ALICE: I have been up here for hours and no one, except you, even noticed I was gone, let alone, came to look for me.

RANDALL: NOOO!! You are wrong!!! That's NOT RIGHT.

ALICE: You're right that's not right. It's WRONG!! It's WRONG PARENTING!!

RANDALL: I—I—CAN'T BELIEVE—I CAN'T BELIEVE . . .

ALICE: BELIEVE IT, RANDY!!

RANDALL: I don't believe . . . in them, any more. I can't—I can't . . .

He stands.

ALICE: Randall, what are you doing? Sit down.

RANDALL: I'm flunking precalc.

ALICE: Randy. Stop. It's okay.

RANDALL: "Okay?" "OKAY?" It's not okay! And I'm not doing well. I am not doing well at all. Our parents don't love us. Tell me our parents love us.

ALICE: I can't.

RANDALL: Listen . . .

They listen.

ALICE: They're fighting again.

RANDALL *goes over to the edge of the roof and jumps off.*

RANDY!!!! NO!!!! RANDY!!! MAMA!!! DADDY!!!!! MA-MAAAAAAA!!!!! DADDY!!!!!!!!!!

Blackout.

END OF PLAY

TEAM B.L. OR DOING THE LIGHTNING BOLT!

Alex Broun

TEAM B.L. or Doing the Lightning Bolt was first produced on November 10, 2012, by Saint Elizabeth's Catholic Primary School at St. Andrew's Church Hall, Richmond, Hampshire, United Kingdom. The production was directed by Sylvie Sice.

CHARACTERS

STEPHANIE: *the team captain.*

LAUREN: *the best player.*

COURTNEY: *the goalkeeper.*

ALEXIS: *a forward.*

VICTORIA: *a defender.*

BRIANNA: *a winger.*

(All characters can be played by actors between the ages of 12 and 16.)

TIME

Day

SETTING

A girls' dressing room.

> *Dressing room. Day. Lights up. A girls soccer team enters after a disappointing loss. They are hot and sweaty and dressed in the team's uniform. Some sit on benches, others take off their cleats and throw them on the floor. LAUREN sits in the corner and takes off her cleats.*

VICTORIA: Well that was great. Congratulations to us. Double congratulations to us. We were hopeless. How hopeless do you have to be? One goal. All we needed was one goal and we couldn't even score that.

BRIANNA: We wouldn't have needed one goal if you hadn't let them score.

VICTORIA: I didn't let them score. Courtney did.

COURTNEY: Only because you let their captain shoot.

VICTORIA: You still could have saved it. It was an easy shot. Their keeper would have saved it.

ALEXIS: Their keeper was good.

VICTORIA: Better than our keeper. If we had their keeper we would have won for sure.

BRIANNA: And their forward. Alexis missed an open goal.

ALEXIS: Their defender tripped me.

BRIANNA: Which defender? The "Invisible girl?"

ALEXIS: Well, we would have scored if you didn't hog the ball all the time.

STEPHANIE: Stop it, Alexis. We all feel bad. It wasn't anybody's fault. We all played badly.

VICTORIA: Lauren didn't. She won Best on Field.

BRIANNA: Lauren always wins Best on Field.

VICTORIA: Then why do we always lose? We have the best player so we should win.

STEPHANIE: That's not always what happens, Vicky. You know that.

VICTORIA: No I don't. We practice just as hard as every other team, we have the same number on the field, we have the best player. We should win. I'm sick and tired of losing.

BRIANNA: And we're sick and tired of you whining all the time.

STEPHANIE: Okay, we lost badly—it doesn't mean we have to be bad losers.

ALEXIS: But we practiced the Lightning Bolt for when we scored and we didn't even get to do it.

STEPHANIE: That's just what happens. Sometimes you win, sometimes you lose.

VICTORIA: No, we lose all the time. We dream of sometimes.

BRIANNA: I dream of you being on another team.

VICTORIA: If I was on another team, we'd beat you as well.

STEPHANIE: Cool it! Everybody cool it. Just calm down. Now I know everybody's upset, I'm upset too.

COURTNEY: You said we'd win.

ALEXIS: You promised we'd win.

VICTORIA: You said if we trained really hard and did everything you said . . .

COURTNEY: We'd win.

BRIANNA: And we did everything you said . . .

ALEXIS: And we still lost.

STEPHANIE: I know you trained really hard and you stuck to the game plan and I'm really grateful for that.

VICTORIA: It would help if we had a coach.

STEPHANIE: Mr. Earnshaw's wife is sick. You know that. He promised he'd come back when she was better.

BRIANNA: When will that be?

STEPHANIE: I don't know. It's just the way it goes. It was a close game but the ball didn't bounce our way.

ALEXIS: Actually it did bounce our way. It bounced right into our goal.

VICTORIA: *To Courtney.* Because she didn't save it.

STEPHANIE: Stop it.

BRIANNA: We were meant to be like Team USA.

ALEXIS: Instead we were Team BL—Big Losers.

STEPHANIE: Stop it!

VICTORIA: There's no color for the medal we won.

COURTNEY: There isn't even a color.

STEPHANIE: STOP IT! Everybody just stop it. We lost, okay, it doesn't matter what anybody says now we lost. Nothing's going to change that. So stop talking. Everybody stop talking! The Olympics is meant to inspire a generation. And we're that generation. So we just have to accept the loss and see what we can learn for next week. We have to work harder. Get better. Just like Team USA.

VICTORIA: That's what you say every week.

STEPHANIE: But it's still true. If we want to do the Lightning Bolt, then we have to be like Usain Bolt. We have to train harder, longer, smarter. You think when he was growing up in Barbados, he had it easy?

LAUREN: *Quietly.* Jamaica.

STEPHANIE: He probably had setbacks just like we did . . .

LAUREN: *Loudly.* Jamaica.

STEPHANIE: But he kept going. And now look at him, he's the . . .

LAUREN: *Louder.* Jamaica.

They all turn to look at LAUREN.

Usain Bolt was born in Jamaica. Not Barbados.

STEPHANIE: Sorry, Jamaica. I meant Jamaica, but it doesn't change the fact that—

LAUREN: *Standing.* In the one hundred meters final, there were three runners from Jamaica—Usain Bolt, Yohan Blake, and Asafa Powell. There were no runners from Barbados. The only runner from Barbados was Ramon Gittens and he got knocked out in the heats.

VICTORIA: Yeah, Stephanie.

LAUREN: And Victoria, you don't have too much to talk about. You did let their captain into the area. But Courtney, it was an easy shot—you should have saved it. And Brianna, you need to pass the ball more, but Alexis did miss an open goal. It was all our faults. Every single one of us.

STEPHANIE: You were the best . . .

LAUREN: Every single one. *Beat.* You know what happened when Usain Bolt went to his first big track meet?

VICTORIA: He won?

ALEXIS: He killed them?

BRIANNA: He left the other runners lying in the mud?

LAUREN: He didn't even make the final. And you know what happened the following year?

ALEXIS: He won.

LAUREN: He got arrested. When he was meant to be preparing for his race, he hid in the back of a van as a practical joke. The police didn't find it so funny though, and he was arrested. They even blamed his coach.

COURTNEY: I didn't know that.

LAUREN: Most people don't. And then in 2004 at the Athens Olympics, he was eliminated in the first round. No one had even heard of him back then. It wasn't till 2008 when he won the gold medal in both the one hundred and two hundred meters in Beijing that he became famous.

BRIANNA: And that's when he did the Lightning Bolt.

All except STEPHANIE *and* LAUREN *dance around doing the Lightning Bolt, a la Usain Bolt.*

LAUREN: No, he didn't. He invented the Lightning Bolt years before. And you know why?

ALEXIS: So he could win?

LAUREN: So he remembers to do the most important thing.

COURTNEY: There's something more important than winning?

LAUREN: Having fun! When he ran in the Junior World Championships in Jamaica in 2002 he got so nervous being in front of his home crowd he put his shoes on the wrong feet. So from that day on he vowed never to let himself be affected by nerves again and just have fun. Don't you see him when he's running? He has a big smile on his face. He loves it. And that's why he runs. And that's why we don't win. Because we don't enjoy it. Look at you all out on the field. Frowning and angry. Stop yelling at each other and have fun. That's when we'll win. And even if we don't win, then it's okay—because at least we had fun. We need to start having fun or else . . .

STEPHANIE: What?

LAUREN: Or else I don't want to play anymore.

ALL *(except Lauren)*: No!

COURTNEY: Please, Lauren.

ALEXIS: You have to play.

VICTORIA: Or then we'll really be Team BL.

LAUREN: Then you all have to swear, right now.

BRIANNA: We swear.

LAUREN: Whatever the result, we have fun.

Holding out her hand, palm facing down.

Agreed?

ALEXIS: *Putting her hand on top of Lauren's.* Agreed.

BRIANNA: *Adding her hand.* Agreed.

COURTNEY: *And hers.* Agreed.

VICTORIA: *And hers.* Agreed.

STEPHANIE: *Adding her hand.* Agreed.

ALL: *Raising their hands.* Team USA!!!

LAUREN: Good. Now there's only one thing to do.

BRIANNA: What's that?

LAUREN: The Lightning Bolt.

They all do the Lightning Bolt as they dance off stage.

END OF PLAY

THE STAR-SPANGLED WOOLY BULLY

Steve Koppman

Inspired by Richard Cohen

The Star-Spangled Wooly Bully by Steve Koppman was originally produced as part of the Eight Tens at Eight Festival at the Actors' Theatre of Santa Cruz, 1001 Center Street, Santa Cruz, CA, January 11 through February 17, 2002. The play was directed by Greg Paroff. The cast was as follows:

ED FISHMAN: Jeff Dinnell
"ITCHY" MITCHIE: Eric Callero
FAITH ROTHSTEIN: Jackie Rubin
ELISE ROTHSTEIN: Amanda James
LINDA MOSS: Leah Harshaw
ED'S FATHER (offstage voice): Greg Paroff

CHARACTERS
ED FISHMAN: *15*
MITCH: *15; gangly, funny looking, and disheveled.*
FAITH ROTHSTEIN: *15*
LINDA MOSS: *14*
ELISE ROTHSTEIN: *13; FAITH's sister.*
ED'S FATHER *(offstage voice)*

TIME
Late 1960s. Summer. After sunset.

SETTING
A quiet street in a Queens, New York City, neighborhood. A churchyard fence is nearby.

> *Front stoop of a two-story brick house. Sounds of yelling offstage.*

ED: *(From offstage.)* Dad.

FATHER: *(From offstage.)* Don't "Dad" me. You've got to be up at four in the morning to catch that bus. When are you ever going to grow up?

> ED *throws open, then slams shut, the front door behind himself, sits on the stoop, and turns on his transistor radio. "Wooly Bully" by Sam the Sham and the Pharaohs plays. Enter* MITCH, *carrying a ukulele; his leg is bleeding, he is sweating profusely, his shirt half out of his pants, his fly half open.* MITCH *strums and bangs the instrument as he sings along roughly in a hoarse, grating voice, changing the words.*

MITCH: Mammy told Laddy 'bout a thing to do, Da-da-di-da-da-be, Come on, learn to screw!

Wooly bully, Wooly bully, Wooly bully!

Mammy told Laddy 'bout a thing she saw, two-bit whore and a woolly dog!

Wooly bully, Wooly bully, Wooly bully!

Speaking. Ay, Fishman. You still wanna be in our band?

ED: Still? Me? What band?

MITCH: You got a great voice, man! I hear you singin' "The Star-

Spangled Banner" in assembly. *Chuckles.* You got resonance, man.

ED: Thanks.

MITCH: We could be the coolest band in the neighborhood, man. Kill the Brittle People. Kick those guys' asses up and down Northern Boulevard. Think of the chicks, man. The chicks!

ED: I don't know.

MITCH: That's the trouble with you, man. You gotta seize the time! You wanna lie on your parents' stoop the rest of your life? Think of it, man. *Eyes wide.* The chicks! Just waitin' for us. You're gonna be eighteen—the peak of your sexual career—in just a coupla years.

ED: What do you call this group anyway?

MITCH: *Shaking his head.* We're changin' our name, man.

ED: What is it?

MITCH: *Sheepishly.* Okay, so we've formerly been—the "Rear Ends." Wanted somethin', you know, a little cooler. Dig this: The Peace Feelers. Like, from Hanoi? But it's got two meanings. Piece . . . Feelers. Get it? *Beat.* Think of it, man. Your name in lights. Or at least on blackboards. "Ed Fishman, Lead Singer." Play the Spring Dance. Make some bread. Be a big man in the neighborhood. And—most of all, man . . .

ED: The chicks.

MITCH: Right on! You dig Faith Rothstein, right? Skanky little broad. No tits but cute. Nice ass. Nice person. Good sense of humor. *Nodding seriously.* Not bad at all.

ED: She's going with Mickey.

MITCH: That don't mean shit, man, believe me. She don't look to me like a one-man woman . . . *Winking.* . . . if you know what I mean.

ED: What happened to your leg? That looks bad.

MITCH: Ran into a damn fire hydrant with my bike, man. Gotta keep your eyes on the road. Not the . . .

BOTH: Chicks!

ED: You think I could really be in your band? Such as it is, I mean.

MITCH: Okay, so you could use a little work on your image, man, if you know what I mean. There's a lot of image in music. You probably don't think I should talk. Ha-ha. I mean, like, you could let your hair grow a little. *Beat.* Who am I kidding? We're a royal bunch of losers. You'd fit right in. Like a fuckin' glove, man. *Beat.* So how's your summer goin'?

ED: *Downbeat.* I've got to go to camp tomorrow morning. My dad got me a job as a waiter. I couldn't be in your group till fall.

MITCH: Hey—it just so happens, don't think we got that many gigs in July and August. I'll check my calendar when I get back to the office. Maybe I'll even call our agent. *Beat.* Things've been a little slow lately. Maybe it's the weather, man.

ED: Camp's gonna be hell. I can't even swim.

MITCH: Why you goin'?

ED: My parents don't want me lying around the house another summer reading. I don't really know what happened. They got me to sign something and now I'm dead meat.

MITCH: Look at the bright side. What's there lots of at camp, man?

ED: They'll really go for a guy who's scared of the water. I'll tell you the truth—I hate camp. I hate the water. I even hate the bus to get there.

MITCH: You could learn to swim, man! Little kids swim! Even retarded ones! You're a genius, man! You could learn that.

ED: Last time I took a swim test, I almost drowned. You know I can't do a forward roll in gym. All that kind of stuff scares the hell out of me, I dunno why. You always have to take a test first thing up there. Look—I can float in shallow water. So, I should be able to jump in, float near the top, then bring on my . . . ED *makes crawling motions.* . . . crawl, right?

MITCH: I dunno, man. Swimming's more like keepin' a beat, ridin' like a bike. I'll tell you a secret, man. You can't tell anybody this, okay? I can swim, but I'm scared shitless of jumpin' into the water. I had to take a test at Scout Camp. On the dock, it's like I'm lookin' down from the Empire State. I hadn't eaten all day. I'm sweatin' like a pig, man. Everybody's yelling and laughing and screamin' "Jump!" Then it's black, it's like I'm dreamin', back home in bed in the mornin' or somethin'. I hit the water like I'm fallin' from a plane and smash through the lake like it's glass. I'm wide awake, thrashing, water pourin' up my throat, it's freezing, I'm coughin', I'm back up there, I can't see anybody, I'm like all alone, like I landed on the wrong planet and then—who do you think I see?

ED: Chicks?

MITCH: No, man. Ha-ha-ha. My counselor wavin' at me, Get your crazy ass over here. I turn around and swim the fifty yards to the far dock. I never swam so good in my life. The sun was so bright and I was like a fish—a fish, man, with arms. It was fucking beautiful. *Beat.* You gotta' ride it, man. All you need is the confidence, man—you got the spirit. I know by the way you sing in Assembly.

ED: We're gonna sing "The Star-Spangled Banner" at the Spring Dance?

MITCH: Why not, man? Look at fuckin' Hendrix. It doesn't matter what you sing. Take a bunch of losers who can't sing, can't play instruments, don't know music from the sound the subway makes over Roosevelt Avenue — and what have you got? The Beatles, man. Bunch of limeys couldn't even comb their hair. The chicks went wild. Shit!

Enter girls, FAITH, LINDA, and ELISE. ED pulls his glasses out of his pocket to look at them. The girls laugh. He stuffs them back in.

FAITH: We're having a party. Wanna come?

LINDA: Oh, Faith!

MITCH: Man, I'm gonna take off. Give you some room.

He sits on the curb, stage left, as if preparing to leave, singing badly.

Can't you understand what I'm tryin' to say,

Can't you feel the feelings I'm feelin' today?

Nah, you don't believe we're on the eve of seduction.

ED: *To* FAITH. How've you been?

FAITH: Everything's boring, boring as usual.

LINDA: Boring, boring.

Girls repeat "boring" like in a round. FAITH waves a cup of Italian ices. ELISE and LINDA start throwing a multicolored ball to each other, which they continue to do intermittently through subsequent action.

FAITH: Everything's so much fun. *Beat. To* MITCH: Itchy Mitchie?

MITCH: Oh, okay, Faith, hi.

FAITH: Hurt yourself?

MITCH: That's okay, man.

ED: *Resuming, to* FAITH. You hear from anybody?

FAITH: Everybody's going completely crazy.

LINDA: *Making circular motions with her finger near* FAITH*'s head.* She means she's crazy.

FAITH: Have you seen the way Suzy's dressing? Her parents are talking about separating and she's pretty crazy.

ED: I haven't seen her.

FAITH: Candy's back from California.

ED: I didn't know she'd gone.

FAITH: She's quite a changed person. She has a boyfriend out there now. An older man. Sixteen. She talks about grass and hippies and acid all the time. She's so cool and sophisticated. It's like everyone's gone loony.

ELISE: *To* ED. But you're someone Faith can depend on.

ED: How's Mickey?

FAITH: I wouldn't write him. He can barely read anyway.

ED: B—B—But you—you were going together.

FAITH: We are not. I'm too young to go steady.

ED: I thought you liked him. Everybody said.

FAITH: I like lots of people. Everybody knows so much.

ED: I wish I knew what they know.

FAITH: They just act like they know everything.

ED: How do they do that?

FAITH: That's what they know that you don't know.

ED: How do you learn?

FAITH: *Shrugging and laughing.* I don't know, Eddie. Maybe it's inborn.

LINDA: *Stepping between* ED *and* FAITH. What are you two lovebirds talking about?

FAITH: Shut up, Linda Corey Moss.

ELISE: *To* FAITH. Show him how you clean your ear out with a pen!

FAITH: Shut up, you.

> *She chases* ELISE, *then pretends to choke her.* ELISE, *screaming, throws a ball wildly over the fence. A dog starts barking.*

Now you've lost our favorite ball. A family *(She mispronounces the word "heirloom.")* hair-loom.

ELISE: *To* FAITH. I got that from Grandma for my birthday. Boo-hoo on you.

FAITH: *To* LINDA. You didn't catch it.

LINDA: It wasn't much more than twenty feet over my head.

MITCH *limps over to the fence, tries to climb, grimaces. He cannot climb.*

MITCH: I must've pulled my leg. I can hardly walk.

FAITH: I've got heels. And you can hardly see in there now. It's too dark.

LINDA: I'd need sneakers. You'd need to know your way around.

MITCH: Guess we've only got one able-bodied man who knows this churchyard well enough to find his way in the dark.

ED: *Whispering, to* MITCH. I've never climbed a fence in my life. I can't.

MITCH: *Whispering back.* There's a first time for everything, man. Just last year, would you believe I'd never picked up a ukulele? Good practice for tomorrow. You can do it. I'll talk you through it. What's the worst that can happen? I'll break your fall.

ED: You can't break my fall on the other side.

MITCH: If you get hurt, you won't even have to go to camp. And guess . . . MITCH *indicates* FAITH, *his eyes bulging* . . . who'd take care of you all summer long. This is what it's all about! Mister lead singer! Mister Olympic swimmer!

> *Dog barks.*

ED: There's a dog in there.

MITCH: Just a little dog. A church dog, man. It's religious.

Dog barks again, louder.

Probably blind.

ED: You're crazy. Why do you think they call you Itchy Mitchie? I can't do this! *Beat.* I thought you were going home, anyway.

ED *and* MITCH *look at the girls.*

MITCH: It's a moment of truth, man. This is what it's all about. She's dependin' on you. And once you're on top of that fence, man, I guarantee, I don't care how scared you are, you'll never feel so free in your life.

Turning to FAITH, *quietly, nervously.*

I don't know how to put this, but maybe our man here needs a little incentive, if you know what I mean.

The girls giggle.

FAITH: No, what do you mean, Mitch?

MITCH: Well—I don't know—like, maybe, if you offered to—I don't know—maybe, like, go out with him—or like, maybe, I don't know, like maybe kiss him or something—maybe that could help make him a little more decisive. I'm not saying what you should do or nothin'. I'm just sayin'—it might . . .

FAITH: I guess I'd go out with Ed if he got our ball.

ED: *Positioning himself to climb the fence, to* MITCH. Tell me exactly what to do. Go real slow. Don't leave out a thing.

Dog barks.

MITCH: Put your foot into one of the little openings. Pull yourself up and fit your other foot into another one of the little openings. Then pull yourself up a little more.

Lights dim. Lights rise. Girls lie on lawn. ED *is on fence or offstage.*

Then you pull yourself up a little more.

ED: *His voice shaking, out of breath.* I'm almost on top. I can't believe this. Oh, God.

MITCH: Don't wanna rush you, man, but one of the chicks fell asleep, and I think I see some gray hairs growin' on the little one.

ED: I can't believe you put me up to this. It's so high up here. I'm going to fall and kill myself. Then I'm going to kill you.

MITCH: Thank me later, man. Just whatever you do, don't look down. You see a metal bar?

ED: Kind of.

MITCH: Now this is the hardest part. Don't look down. Take hold of the bar. Swing your foot over.

ED: Oh, my God! Look how far down it is! I'm so scared. I'm gonna fall any minute. God, Mitch, I gotta get down!

Dog starts barking hysterically.

MITCH: You already made it, man. You're up there. You said you couldn't do it. Listen to me. Just swing your foot over the bar like you're sittin' on a horse.

ED: I never rode a horse. Oh God. Oh God!

MITCH: Like you're sittin' on anything. But before you do—I got a friendly word of advice. *Beat.* Watch out for your balls, man. You cut your balls on the fence, it kills the whole damn evening. Heh-heh-heh. Now, once you're sitting, swing your other leg over.

ED: *Panting.* I can't do this. Oh God. Oh God. Oh God.

MITCH: Which part didn't you get?

ED: I gotta get down. I'm gonna fall. It's so far down. I'm so scared. Oh God. Oh God.

MITCH: You're not gonna fall, man. Stay cool. Everybody feels like this. You're practically there.

The fence shakes. Dog barks.

Stay cool, man!

ED: AAAAAHHHHHH!

He crashes to ground, knocking MITCH *over. Long pause.*

MITCH: Okay, so you blew it, man. *Beat.* But—wasn't it worth the try?

ED: Maybe . . . Maybe it was.

LINDA: She never said she wouldn't go out with you if you didn't make it over the stupid fence.

FAITH: Shut up, Linda Corey Moss!

MITCH: Well, I tell you, I gotta split, man. I gotta work in the mornin'. Good luck at camp.

Shakes hands with ED.

ED: I'll be okay. Maybe I can still miss the bus.

All the rest wave good-bye and exit. ED *limps down the dark street toward his stoop. He's bruised and his clothes are torn, but he's smiling and humming "Wooly Bully." In front of his house, he makes out his father standing, offstage, in darkness.*

FATHER: *From offstage.* Where have you been all this time? Where'd you go with those girls?

ED *tries to speak but no words come out.*

Answer me. We didn't know where you were. You've got to get up at four in the morning. When the hell are you ever going to grow up?

END OF PLAY

WHITE BRA WITH A PINK BOW

Charlene A. Donaghy

White Bra with a Pink Bow premiered on March 16, 2013, and was produced by the New Urban Theatre Laboratory at Boston SWAN (Support Women Arts Now) Day, Massachusetts, under the direction of Jackie Davis, with the following cast:

BECCA: Jojo Kindair
TAMMY: Alycia Love-Modeste
KIM: Tasia A. Jones

Produced at the Warner International Playwrights Festival
October 17–19, 2013
Featuring:

Marie Roy-Daniels as BECCA
Elizabeth Keiser as TAMMY
Laura Honeywood as KIM

CHARACTERS

BECCA, *a shy 13-year-old. She is wearing a pair of 1972-era gym shorts and a top.*

TAMMY, *a boisterous 13-year-old. She is wearing a pair of 1972-era gym shorts and a top.*

KIM, *an athletic 13-year-old. She is wearing a pair of bell-bottoms and a vintage New Orleans sports team T-shirt.*

TIME

An early autumn afternoon in New Orleans, Louisiana, in September of 1972.

SETTING

Junior high school girl's locker room. A locker room bench is center stage with a gym bag on the floor next to it. A large mirror is set on stage or the fourth wall can act as a mirror.

PRODUCTION NOTES

All actors stay clothed during the play. The "pencil test" segments should be blocked over T-shirts.

Playwright gives permission for play personalization with city/town of production. Approved changes are: KIM'S vintage T-shirt to a local team, changing "Pontchartrain Park" to a local 1970s-era park hangout, and changing "D. H. Holmes" to a local 1970s-era department store.

Set and lighting can be simplified to fit minimalist staging elements.

> *In darkness, a locker room shower is overheard. Blue lights cascade onto the stage like shower water, turning white, then filling the stage with full light. BECCA stands in front of the mirror looking at herself, singing a line or two from a song like "Walking in the Rain" by the Partridge Family. Shower fades. BECCA moves her hands to her breasts, which are already developed far beyond those of her friends.*

BECCA: I have to grow up, please let me have little boobs like Laurie Partridge.

> *TAMMY enters, snaps a towel at BECCA.*

TAMMY: Ha! You'll never have Laurie Partridge boobs, birthday girl. You're already too big.

BECCA: Nut-uh!

TAMMY: Yeah-huh! You could entertain the troops in Vietnam with . . .

BECCA: I wish I could go there.

TAMMY: Becca, I'm your best friend, right?

> BECCA *nods.*

It'd be far out if somebody could fix this, but you can't live only for that day. Your dad wouldn't want you to. We're in eighth grade. Junior high top of the heap. And look at you. You need a bra! What a great birthday present!

BECCA: If I need a bra, that means I can't stay ten years old. I promised I'd stay a little girl.

TAMMY: We haven't been ten years old . . .

BECCA: In three years.

TAMMY: We're teenagers now. We're gonna go to eighth-grade dances at Pontchartrain Park. With boys!

BECCA: I don't need any boys.

TAMMY: Yeah-huh. Can't stop time even if we wanna. Boobs are gonna grow . . . well, maybe not mine. *Beat.* If you can put a pencil under your boob and it stays, you need a bra.

BECCA: Who says?

TAMMY: All the ninth graders.

BECCA: Nut-uh.

TAMMY: Yeah-huh.

BECCA: Nut-uh.

TAMMY: Let's try.

BECCA: No.

TAMMY: Don't be a spaz. C'mon.

> *She rummages through gym bag, grabs a pencil, sticks it under her breast (see production note). It falls, clattering to floor. Beat. They stare at it.*

TAMMY: Bogus. Your turn.

BECCA: No!

TAMMY *grabs at* BECCA *who turns away.* TAMMY *tickles* BECCA, *who finally giggles and tickles her back.*

Laughing. Stop it.

TAMMY: *Laughing.* C'mon, Laurie Partridge!

BECCA: *Laughing.* Stop. Stop! Okay.

She takes the pencil and places it under her breast (see production note). It stays. Beat. They stare in the mirror.

TAMMY: Neat! It's like it's glued there.

BECCA *removes the pencil and hands it to* TAMMY.

I'm sorry I said that. About Vietnam, I mean.

KIM *enters carrying her gym outfit and a tennis racket.*

KIM: Our first gym class of eighth grade, and they cancel it. At least we got to change. Did you see the new girl from California? She's looks like a surfer girl. Tan with the longest hair I've ever seen. I wonder if she plays tennis.

She puts her gym outfit in the gym bag and swings the tennis racket.

Billie Jean King is playing Karry Melville Saturday. King is gonna rule. Be there or be square. Happy birthday, Becs.

TAMMY: Becca needs a bra.

KIM: What's that gotta to do with tennis?

TAMMY: Nothing. I'm just saying. We did the pencil test. *Pause.* Here's your pencil.

Tosses pencil to KIM.

Becca's lucky.

BECCA: Nut-uh.

TAMMY: Yeah-huh! Every boy in school is gonna wanna date you. It's like you grew watermelons this summer.

BECCA: I'm not getting a bra!

KIM: Who cares what boys want, anyway?

She tries to put the pencil under her breast (see production note) but it keeps falling back into her hand. She finally throws it into her gym bag.

BECCA: My dad said I'll always be his girl. I don't need any boys.

TAMMY: I'd faint if someone like David Cassidy would just look at me. Did you see him on the cover of *Tiger Beat* last week? It was 1972 Super Sweethearts Issue. He was wearing a leather jacket, sitting on a motorcycle. He's so bitchin'.

BECCA: I hate motorcycles.

TAMMY: Motorcycles are bitchin'.

KIM: Nobody's gonna wanna date you if you say "bitchin'."

TAMMY: Okay. Cool. Is that what California girl would say?

> *She sticks her tongue out at* KIM. KIM *reciprocates.*

BECCA: See. We don't have to grow up.

> *She sticks her tongue out at* TAMMY *and* KIM.

TAMMY: Yeah-huh. Let's go buy you a bra. We'll get something like in the back of the J. C. Penney catalog . . .

BECCA: Tam . . .

TAMMY: Where the women have black bras or . . .

BECCA: Tam!

TAMMY: Ones with leopard spots or something with lace . . .

BECCA: Tammy!

TAMMY: You're gonna be so popular. We're gonna rule junior high, and by the time we get to be freshmen . . .

BECCA: Tammy!

TAMMY: What?

BECCA: I. Don't. Want. A. Bra!

KIM: We can't buy bras at J. C. Penney, anyways. What do you think, there's some magic box where you can, I don't know, find anything you wish for, point to it and it'll magically appear at your door?

BECCA: If I could do that, I'd wish for something other than a stupid bra. Besides, we're thirteen. My mom would have to drive us to Penney's.

TAMMY: Bitch . . . I mean, cool.

KIM: Your mom has leopard bras. She even has red ones. And purple.

TAMMY: *Teasing.* Spying?

KIM: Nut-uh. She washes 'em and hangs 'em in the bathroom. To dry.

BECCA: I don't want leopard or red or purple! If I have to have a stupid bra, then I want one of those white ones with a pink bow in the middle. I'll bet Laurie Partridge wears a white one with a pink bow in the middle.

TAMMY: Boring!

BECCA: Nut-uh.

TAMMY: Yeah-huh.

BECCA: Nut-uh!

TAMMY: Yeah-huh! And I'm tellin' ya, leather-wearing boys want girls with leopard bras.

BECCA: I don't want leather-wearing boys.

TAMMY: I am not going to the eighth-grade dances with you two. You're gonna have to get dates eventually. And you could have any boy in school.

BECCA: I'd want somebody like . . .

TAMMY: Like?

KIM: Why do we only talk about boys, lately?

TAMMY: Cuz we're supposed to talk about boys.

KIM: Not me.

TAMMY: Ever?

KIM *sticks her tongue out at* TAMMY.

Hope your face freezes that way.

BECCA: Like my dad.

TAMMY: You want her face to freeze like your dad?

BECCA: I wanna boy like my dad. Somebody who's brave and strong and will take me to Dairy Queen for Dilly Bars and listen to the Partridge Family with me. His last letter said they're his favorite band, too.

KIM: They're gonna find him. He's a pilot. He is brave and strong.

BECCA: The Air Force keeps telling us that. *Beat.* I don't think my mom wants him found. She never had leopard bras or rode motorcycles before he went to Vietnam.

KIM: Maybe she did and you just didn't know.

BECCA: Somewhere he's wishing on stars to come home. I know it. He has to be.

KIM: Sure he is.

BECCA: And I don't wanna date boys or grow up. I wanna be exactly like he remembers me.

TAMMY: He'd want you to grow up. Be a teenager. You can date somebody like Michael Jackson. It'll be . . .

She sings a line from a song like The Jackson Five's "A-B-C." KIM then joins in and they both sing a line. BECCA *then joins in and all three sing a line. They giggle.*

And we'll bicycle over to D. H. Holmes and get you a white bra with a pink bow. Okay?

BECCA: Do I have to?

TAMMY *nods.* BECCA *nods slowly with her.*

KIM: It'll be okay. I can maybe ask the new girl to go with us.

TAMMY: Nut-uh. *Pause.* But can I at least try on a leopard bra?

KIM: For your mosquito bites?

BECCA *giggles.*

Lights fade.

END OF PLAY